THE HEALTH BENEFITS OF MEDICINAL MUSHROOMS

Mark Stengler, N.D.

Basic
Health
PUBLICATIONS, INC.

The information contained in this book is based upon the research and personal and professional experiences of the author. It is not intended as a substitute for consulting with your physician or other healthcare provider. Any attempt to diagnose and treat an illness should be done under the direction of a healthcare professional.

The publisher does not advocate the use of any particular healthcare protocol but believes the information in this book should be available to the public. The publisher and author are not responsible for any adverse effects or consequences resulting from the use of the suggestions, preparations, or procedures discussed in this book. Should the reader have any questions concerning the appropriateness of any procedures or preparation mentioned, the author and the publisher strongly suggest consulting a professional healthcare advisor.

Editor: Carol Rosenberg
Typesetter: Gary A. Rosenberg
Cover Designer: Mike Stromberg

Basic Health Guides are published by
Basic Health Publications, Inc.

ISBN: 978-1-59120-143-4 (Pbk.)
ISBN: 978-1-68162-808-0 (Hardcover)

Contents

Introduction

The use of supplemental forms of medicinal mushrooms has gained tremendous popularity among nutrition-oriented practitioners and consumers over the past decade. Centuries of use by Asian herbalists and doctors, solid scientific research, and growing reports in the popular press all have helped to create an explosion of interest in the health benefits offered by mushroom supplements.

Much of this excitement has been generated by clinical research showing mushroom extracts restoring immune competency and improving outcome for people with a variety of serious illnesses, including cancer, hepatitis, asthma, and other conditions where effective nontoxic treatment options are limited.

However, while the health benefits of mushroom supplements are many, "mushroom supplements" as found in the marketplace refer to a large and chemically diverse group of products, very few of which match the potency of the mushroom remedies used in traditional herbalism or the mushroom supplements used in the clinical research, including the research showing immune benefit for chronic illness. Picking the supplement that matches the potency and quality of the supplements used in the supporting research requires that several key issues about medicinal mushroom supplements be understood. This understanding is important if people are to achieve the health benefits and therapeutic results identified in the clinical research and described in the popular literature.

The first issue to consider is the relationship between manufacturing methods and product quality and potency. According to the world's leading mushroom experts, the method by which a mushroom supplement is manufactured is critically important to creating the potency needed to achieve the health benefits identified in traditional herbalism and the clinical research. The majority of published scientific literature that I was able to locate on the clinical effects and health benefits of using medicinal mushrooms used supplements prepared with hot-water extraction. This is also consistent with the references on traditional use by East Asian herbalists.

The second issue to review is the importance of understanding the descriptions used on the labels of the many diverse forms of mushroom supplements found in your local health food stores and pharmacies. Understanding product descriptions and how they relate to the potency of a product ties into the first issue of manufacturing methods and product quality, helping you to find the potency you need for the benefit you seek.

Many of the primary active compounds in medicinal mushrooms are well known, and research has established the levels needed for prevention and therapeutic benefit. People should be looking for precise potency information on supplement labels and recommended potency levels for all the mushrooms discussed later in the book.

Finally, I will summarize the most common supplemental medicinal mushrooms and their best clinical uses. The goal of this book is to give you the information you need to be an expert on mushroom supplements when you walk into your local health food store. You will be able to choose the mushroom supplement that conforms to the quality standards identified in the research and achieve the desired health benefits offered by medicinal mushrooms.

The Nature
of Mushrooms

Fungi are an essential part of a sustainable world. They are involved in the decaying and recycling of matter into the nutrients that animals and plants feed on. Medicinal mushrooms in particular help to purify the environment by decomposing dead trees and plants. For humans, there are approximately 700 species that can be eaten as a nutritious food. And, of course, medicinal mushrooms provide a wide variety of health benefits that can contribute to the prevention and treatment of disease.

What is commonly referred to as a "mushroom" is also called the fruit body. This is the part of the fungus that grows above ground, with the sole purpose of releasing spores (seeds) as part of the reproduction cycle. Some fungi do not produce mushrooms and release their spores without a fruiting body.

The spores of fungi are transported by wind and water to a favorable environment where the spores can germinate and generate a new colony. The new colony begins with the threadlike filaments called "hyphae" that emerge from the germinated spores. The original hyphae continue to grow, seeking another compatible hyphae to mate with. After mating, the hyphae branch out in all directions, colonizing the surrounding soil or decaying tree. This weblike collection of interconnected hyphae is then referred to as the "mycelium."

Mycelium lives year round, expanding and growing beneath the surface of the soil or tree. Mycelium works to acquire food, breaking down organic substances in the surrounding soil and decaying wood. It is tightly packed mycelium that actually

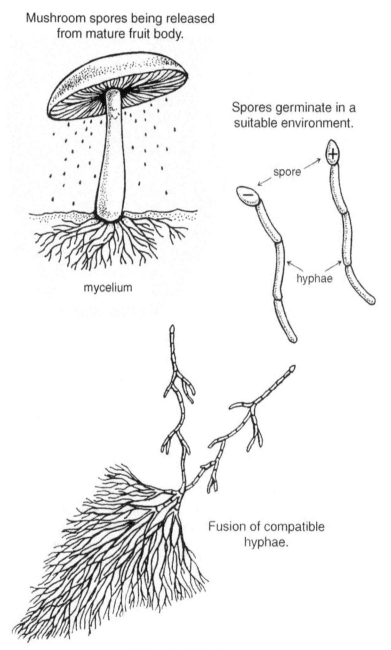

Mushroom spores being released from mature fruit body.

Spores germinate in a suitable environment.

spore

hyphae

mycelium

Fusion of compatible hyphae.

Lifecycle of Mushrooms

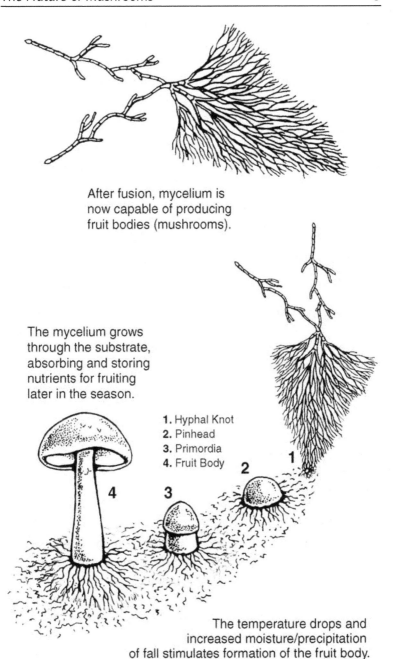

After fusion, mycelium is now capable of producing fruit bodies (mushrooms).

The mycelium grows through the substrate, absorbing and storing nutrients for fruiting later in the season.

1. Hyphal Knot
2. Pinhead
3. Primordia
4. Fruit Body

The temperature drops and increased moisture/precipitation of fall stimulates formation of the fruit body.

forms the fruit body/mushroom we see above the ground or on tree trunks, typically during spring or fall after the seasonal rain and temperature changes. Fungi live near the bottom of the ladder in the ecosystem. Similar to humans they have an immune system to protect against a variety of pathogens. During the mycelial stage, when fungi actively digest food and fight hostile competitors, they excrete digestive enzymes to decompose matter. Before the digested food can be absorbed into the cells where the food is used, the fungi must deactivate pathogens and toxins. This is done by releasing special polysaccharides and other disease-fighting chemicals inside the cell walls where the food passes through. This process is believed to provide many of the nutrients that are also invaluable for the human immune system.

Product Quality and Potency

There appears to be a lot of confusion regarding what standards are essential for a therapeutic "mushroom extract." I feel the best way to address this topic is to review how medicinal mushrooms have been used historically and to examine the published scientific data. Traditional Chinese medicine and the medical research represent nearly our entire experience with medicinal mushrooms. Using these two benchmarks, we found a single theme bridging the gap between centuries of historical use as observed in Chinese medicine and the modern experience of validation through scientific research. This common link is hot-water extraction.

Traditional Use

The traditional use of medicinal mushrooms in Chinese medicine and the herbalism of other cultures is very clear. Mushrooms have always been prepared for medicinal use by hot-water extraction. The extraction was done using heat and water in the process of making teas or decoctions. In a decoction, the herb or mushroom is simmered or boiled in water for a period of time, usually 20 to 120 minutes. This should not be confused with an infusion, where water is poured over the herb. Any practitioner of Oriental medicine will verify that decocting is the historical and current method of preparing medicinal mushrooms for tonic use or immune benefit.

Modern Research

A review of the published scientific literature on medicinal mushrooms demonstrates that the majority of mushroom supplements tested in the medical research were hot-water or hot-water/alcohol extracts. This method is used for the most commonly used mushroom extracts, including coriolus, shiitake, maitake, cordyceps, and reishi. Hot-water extraction is also used for all of the well-known isolate products such as Lentinan and LEM from shiitake, Maitake D-Fraction and MaitakeGold 404® from maitake, and PSK/VPS and PSP from *Coriolus versicolor.*

Breaking Down Cell Walls

Many of the rules for preparing plant-based herbs do not apply to mushroom supplements because mushrooms have a unique structure that is completely different from plants. The cell wall in plants is composed of cellulose while mushrooms have a cell wall made of chitin. Chitin is the same hard fiber contained in the shell of a lobster. This is important since chitin is indigestible by humans; yet chitin contains the potent immune-stimulating compounds common to all medicinal mushrooms, the beta-glucans, specific types of polysaccharides. Hot-water extraction is the only proven method for breaking down the chitinous cell walls and releasing the bioactive polysaccharide structurally intact and undamaged. Also, only a heated liquid solution can concentrate the active compounds into therapeutically effective levels in a bioavailable form. This explains why knowledgeable practitioners of traditional East-Asian medicine and modern clinical researchers and doctors use hot-water extraction to overcome the barrier of indigestible chitin.

Some of the popular literature on medicinal mushrooms has suggested that grinding whole dried mushrooms or mycelium to a powder can break up the indigestible cell walls and "release" the beta-glucans contained inside, allowing for their absorption through the digestive process. However, grinding mushrooms is never recommended in traditional herbalism or the medical research. There are a couple of reasons why this might be the case.

As explained in the next section, many scientists believe that the immune-boosting power of beta-glucans is based on their shape. If the grinding is disruptive enough to break down the cell walls in dried mushrooms or mycelium, it also runs the risk of breaking down the structure and shape of the beta-glucans contained inside. Hot-water extraction, by "melting away" the indigestible chitin that surrounds the beta-glucan, maintains the beta-glucan's original shape and structure.

Also, hot-water extraction allows the indigestible fiber to be removed from the supplement, leaving more room in the capsule for active compounds. Grinding removes nothing, leaving a supplement that may contain primarily indigestible fiber. Capsule for capsule, dehydrated hot-water extracts can be up to thirty times more powerful than mycelium biomass.

The Beta-Glucan Connection

The beta-glucans found inside the cell walls of medicinal mushrooms are a specific type of polysaccharide, and, on average, are far more complex than the molecules found in plants. Unlike plant-based molecules, which provide the molecular blueprints for 80 percent of pharmaceutical drugs, the complex polysaccharides in medicinal mushrooms are difficult to reproduce synthetically.

Mushroom beta-glucans are often referred to as "long chain" molecules or "macro" molecules. They consist of multiple spiraling chains of repeating molecular patterns. The spirals and the different patterns of linking create the complex three-dimensional shapes that give the molecules their names.

The term "beta-glucan" is a classification based on structural characteristics with particular designations such as beta 1-4 or beta 1-3 further describing the linking pattern in the long chain molecule. The glucose structure of the beta-glucans is formed from six carbon atoms. Each of the six carbon atoms in the glucose structure is a potential starting or ending point for the links that bind these long chain molecules together. Beta 1-3 has links going from the first to the third carbon, beta 1-4 from the first to the fourth.

In the 1980s, researchers at Harvard University began to understand how critically important shape and structure were to the immune-boosting power of the beta-glucan molecule. Researchers observed a beta-glucan molecule "linking up" with receptors on the surface of an important immune cell, a macrophage. They observed a classic "lock and key" receptor relationship where the shape of the "key," the beta-glucan structure, is all important. This process was observed to stimulate the macrophage activity and soon after, continued research found other examples.

Receptor sites were found on other immune cells such as natural killer cells and neutrophils, and continued research found that different shaped beta-glucans produced different immune responses, immune responses that dramatically improved outcome for a number of serious medical conditions and diseases.

Are All Mushroom Products Equal?

Interestingly, many of the common mushroom supplements prescribed by practitioners or found in health food stores are not manufactured using hot-water extraction. Liquid alcohol tinctures and unextracted forms such as mycelium biomass and dried mushroom powder have little published data on their effectiveness. An informal survey of retail supplement companies that produce or distribute medicinal mushroom products found that few of these companies had published data to support all of their products. This is not to state unconditionally that alcohol tinctures and unextracted products have no value. However, it would make little sense for any trained practitioner or consumer to use a non-hot-water extract when the benefits are unproven and unknown, especially when the clinically proven hot-water extracts are readily available. This is of particular concern as mushroom supplements tend to be used for serious chronic illnesses such as cancer, hepatitis, chronic fatigue, HIV/AIDS, other immune-deficiency conditions, and cardiovascular disease.

In a monograph on Reishi recently published by the American Herbal Pharmacopoeia, the world's top herbal and medical

MUSHROOM SUPPLEMENT DESCRIPTIONS

There are a number of different types of medicinal mushroom supplements and many names to describe them. The following discussion covers most of the descriptions people are likely to find on the labels of mushroom-based supplements.

Mushroom supplements are made from either the mushroom fruit body or the mushroom mycelium. The efficacy of any of these forms of mushroom supplements, as with other supplements, depends on the strength or potency of the preparation. The research indicates that for mushroom supplements, therapeutic strength requires an extraction process that concentrates the active compounds to levels higher than what is found in the unextracted mushrooms or mycelium. Chinese herbal references usually recommend 6 to 20 grams of dried mushrooms daily (or more), prepared as a tea. The research usually recommends 1 to 4 grams of a concentrated hot-water extract daily.

Unextracted Mushroom Supplements

Mycelium Biomass. Mycelium grown on cereal grain that is dried, powdered, and encapsulated. The levels of active compounds are not listed on the label. This material is typically 50 percent undigested grain, by weight.

experts on the use of medicinal mushrooms discussed the issues associated with non-hot water extracts, including the lack of scientific validation, the potential lack of bio-availability, and the low levels of active compounds.

After reviewing the medical research on Reishi they stated that "a review of these data did not appear to be relevant to the use of mycelium products in the United States." The "findings

---

Mycelium Powder. Mycelium grown in liquid or on grain that is dried, powdered, and encapsulated. The levels of active compounds are not listed on the label.

"Fruit Body" or "Mushroom" Powder. The mature mushroom fruit body dried, ground to a powder, and encapsulated. Levels of active compounds are not listed on the label.

Extracted Mushroom Supplements

Hydro-Alcohol Extract. It can be made from mycelium grown on grain (mycelium biomass), or the mushroom fruit body. Also know as "tinctures," these liquid "extracts" are preserved in grain or grape alcohol. The levels of active compounds are not listed on the label. Most products state that 30 drops is equal to 1 gram of fresh mushroom or mycelium. As a point of comparison, most herbal sources recommend 6–20 grams of dried mushrooms a day, prepared as a tea. It takes 10 grams fresh to make 1 gram dry.

Hot-Water Extract. Can be made from the mycelium or the mushroom fruit body. Usually the extract is dehydrated into a powder and encapsulated (except Maitake Fractions). With this process the levels of active compounds can be concentrated to specific and desired levels. The levels of active compounds are usually listed on the label as a percentage of total weight.

of studies utilizing specific polysaccharides" cannot be used to "substantiate the effectiveness of orally administered commercial reishi mushroom mycelium biomass products because of a potential lack of bio-availability. Lastly, most of the studies reviewed used concentrations of isolated constituents that are magnitudes higher than what is available in crude (unextracted) mycelium biomass preparations."

These experts correctly recognized that the active compounds in unextracted mycelium might still be surrounded by the indigestible chitin. They also acknowledged that the hot-water extraction used to prepare the research supplements created significantly higher levels of active compounds as compared to unextracted supplements.

Although the authors were discussing supplements made from unextracted reishi mycelium, it is important to remember that mushrooms themselves are constructed from tightly packed mycelium. Given the similar structure and shared biology of the medicinal mushrooms and their mycelium, these conclusions likely hold true for all of the non-hot-water extracted mushroom and mycelium supplements.

Nature's Top Seven Medicinal Mushrooms

Medicinal mushrooms are best used based on a person's symptoms and proven clinical uses. In the following chapters, I discuss seven of the most popular medicinal mushrooms and more detailed information on how they work as well as what symptoms/conditions they are most helpful for.

Agaricus blazei

U nlike the other mushrooms covered in this book, *A. blazei* was never used in East Asian herbalism. Instead, it has an extensive history of use as a folk remedy in Brazil. Because this mushroom was heralded by villagers as a longevity tonic, researchers were spurred to take a closer look. This species contains a unique beta-glucan complex that appears to activate many components of the immune system including T lymphocytes, granulocytes, and C3 complement. Animal studies have demonstrated anticancer and antitumor properties. One study also found that *A. blazei* induced apoptosis (self destruction) of malignant cells.

A. blazei has also generated considerable excitement, as some scientists believe it contains the highest levels of beta-glucans among medicinal mushrooms. Although animal and in vitro studies are quite positive, there is a need for more human data.

Supplement Facts

Amount Per Capsule

Agaricus blazei fruit body extract 40% Beta Glucan (polysaccharide)	400 mg*

*Daily Value not established

Minimum potency to look for in *Agaricus blazei.*

Known active constituents: polysaccharides, ergosterols

Clinical Use: Immune modulation, especially in regards to cancer.

Dosage: 1,600–3,200 mg of hot-water extract daily, containing a minimum of 40% polysaccharide (beta-glucan). Take two to four 400-milligram capsules twice daily on an empty stomach.

Safety Profile: Polysaccharides from *A. blazei* are considered nontoxic and safe. As an immune modulator it should be used with extreme care or avoided in organ-transplant patients using immunosuppressive agents.

Cordyceps sinensis

*C*ordyceps sinensis is also called the "caterpillar fungus," as it grows on and acquires nutrients from several species of caterpillars. In China, it is referred to as "winter worm, summer grass." This fungus is found at high altitude in the mountains of China, Nepal, and Tibet.

Cordyceps attracted the attention of the general public and the health profession in 1993 when a group of Chinese runners broke nine world records in the World Outdoor Track and Field Championships in Germany. The coach of these Chinese athletes attributed those results to the athletes regular use of a *Cordyceps*-based tonic. Because *Cordyceps* helps increase stamina, energy levels, and endurance, it has become one of the top-selling sports supplements among the worlds' elite competitive athletes.

In traditional Chinese medicine, *C. sinensis* is considered to benefit the lung and kidney channels. It is commonly used with the elderly in China as a type of "super-ginseng" for rejuvenation and stamina.

Since it is difficult to collect enough *Cordyceps* from the wild, commercial fermentation methods have been developed in China. These methods are now used here in the West to produce it commercially. Cs-4 is an isolated strain of wild *Cordyceps* that has been the focus of much study and is used by clinics throughout China, and recently in the United States.

Important Studies

Cordyceps has several important uses. The following are conditions for which it has been shown effective in studies.

Improves Fatigue

More than 2,000 patients with a variety of medical problems have been involved with clinical trials of Cs-4 extract. Placebo-controlled studies have found *Cordyceps* to benefit elderly patients with fatigue. Subjective improvements included reduced fatigue, cold intolerance, dizziness, nighttime urination, tinnitus, hyposexuality, and amnesia.

Animal studies suggest that *Cordyceps* improves the ability of organs and tissues to use oxygen more efficiently and increases the production of adenosine triphosphate (ATP) for energy.

Adrenal and Sexual Function

Studies have shown *Cordyceps* to have a homeostatic or balancing effect on adrenal hormones and to protect against adrenal atrophy. Many holistic doctors prescribe *Cordyceps* for supporting and regenerating adrenal gland function.

Along the same lines, human studies have demonstrated benefit in patients reporting low libido. For example, in a double-blind, placebo-controlled, clinical trial, patients who reported decreased sex drives were treated with *Cordyceps*. Those receiving the *Cordyceps* had a subjective improvement rate that was significantly higher than those receiving the placebo. Also, the group receiving *Cordyceps* had a much higher increase in 17-ketosteroid in the urine in a twenty-four-hour period (signifying adrenal stimulation) as compared to those who were receiving placebo. *Cordyceps* has been used in traditional Chinese medicine for the treatment of sexual dysfunction and male impotence.

Respiratory Support

Cordyceps also has a long history of use in the natural treatment of chronic respiratory disorders such as asthma, chronic bronchitis, and other respiratory diseases. Various studies have demonstrated positive effects to improve respiratory function. It should be noted that it takes five to six weeks for asthmatics to see improvement, and the benefits require continued use of the supplement. However, cordyceps can be used for long periods of time without a problem.

Kidney Health

This remarkable fungus has been relied upon by physicians in China for benefit in the treatment of chronic kidney diseases such as chronic nephritis, kidney failure, chronic pyelonephritis, and others. Studies also show that it has a protective effect against chemicals toxic to the kidneys. For example, one study of thirty patients with chronic renal failure found treatment with *Cordyceps* resulted in an overall significant improvement in kidney function. A significant increase in creatinine clearance and a significant reduction in BUN (the concentration of nitrogen in the form of urea in the blood) were noted. In addition, there were significant improvements in anemia, with increases in hemoglobin and red blood cell counts.

Cardiovascular Benefits

Human and animal studies have demonstrated a diverse amount of benefits from *Cordyceps* for the cardiovascular system. This includes positive studies regarding its effects on arrhythmias, ischemic heart disease, and chronic heart failure.

Animal and human studies have shown *Cordyceps* to lower total cholesterol, triglycerides, LDL-C, and VLDL-C, and increased HDL-C. A double-blind, randomized, placebo-controlled study, which lasted two months, looked at the effects of *Cordyceps* on elevated cholesterol levels. Over half of the patients on *Cordyceps* therapy had greater than a 10 percent decrease in total cholesterol and more than a 20 percent decrease in triglycerides, while 76 percent of patients had greater than a 10 percent increase in HDL cholesterol.

Interestingly, animal studies have demonstrated that *Cordyceps* can dilate the coronary arteries and increase blood flow to the heart. This circulatory effect has been shown to also occur with the cerebrovascular arteries and blood supply to the brain.

Other Studies

Smaller studies have also shown *Cordyceps* to have potential value in the treatment of hepatitis B and diabetes. *Cordyceps* also has a diverse effect on the immune system. It has been studied in combination with chemotherapy and radiation treatment for lung cancer and patients showed improved tolerance of these therapies with the supplementation of *Cordyceps*.

Supplement Facts

Amount Per Capsule

Cordyceps sinensis Cs-4 mycelium extract   400 mg*
14% Beta Glucan (polysaccharide),
6% cordycepic acid, .15% adenosine

---

*Daily Value not established

Minimum potency to look for in *Cordyceps sinensis*.

Known active constituents: cordycepin, d-mannitol, adenosine, various polysaccharides

Clinical Use: adrenal fatigue, asthma, athlete's foot, cancer, chronic bronchitis, chronic fatigue, chronic renal failure, decreased libido, diabetes, emphysema, heart disease, hepatitis B, hypercholesterolemia, and tinnitus.

Dosage: 800 to 2,400 milligrams of a hot-water/ethanol extract from fermented mycelia of *Cordyceps sinensis*, strain Cs-4, containing a minimum of 14% polysaccharide (beta-glucan), 6% cordycepic acid, and 0.15% adenosine. Take one to three 400-mg capsules twice daily on an empty stomach.

Safety Profile: Extremely safe. As an immune modulator it should be used with extreme care or even avoided in organ transplant patients using immunosuppressive agents.

Coriolus versicolor
(Trametes versicolor)

The most well-studied mushroom extract in the world is without a doubt *Coriolus versicolor*. One of the world's leading anticancer drugs was derived from this mushroom.

More than 400 studies have been published that demonstrate the significant immuno-modulating properties of *C. versicolor* in both healthy people and those affected by chronic conditions. *C. versicolor* is very well known in East Asian medicine, especially in the countries of Japan and China. It has an extensive history of use in both traditional and modern conventional practice.

C. versicolor is found in the United States and throughout the temperate forests of the world. It readily grows on logs or on the injured wood of most kinds of trees. It has woody, fruiting bodies that overlap each other and are found on the sides of stumps and tree trunks. *Coriolus* has a unique, plush, velvety surface that is colored in varying shades of brown or gray, with a distinctive pattern of alternating bands of dark and light color. In the West *Coriolus* is referred to as "turkey tail," due to its fan shaped, multicolored cap. *C. versicolor* is also known as *Trametes versicolor*. The Latin translation of *Trametes* is: "one who is thin" and *versicolor* means "variously colored." In Japan it is called Kawaratake, "the mushroom by the river bank," and in China it is referred to as Yun Zhi, meaning "cloud mushroom." In Japan *Coriolus* has been a folk remedy for cancer and in traditional Chinese medicine it is used to dispel phlegm, and to treat pulmonary infections, hepatitis, and cancer.

Origins

Like many of the mushroom extracts, *Coriolus* has an interesting history with respect to its modern applications. In 1965, a chemical engineer for a pharmaceutical company observed his neighbor with late-stage stomach cancer treating himself with *Coriolus*. The engineer convinced his coworkers to study the mushroom. They eventually developed an extract from the mushroom known as PSK, the abbreviation for Polysaccharide-K. The K stands for the first letter of Kureha Chemical, the company that developed PSK, also known as the anticancer drug Krestin. Krestin went on to become a top-selling cancer drug in Japan. This inspired Chinese researchers to develop their own extract. This was accomplished and it is called PSP, an abbreviation for Polysaccharide-peptide. PSP is slightly different from PSK/VPS. PSP has peptide linked beta-glucans, while PSK/VPS have protein linked by beta-glucans.

Chemistry Profile

Protein-bound polysaccharides are the main focus of *Coriolus*. The main component is a beta-D-glucan. The main chain consists of a 1–4 (beta-glucan, with [1,3] beta-glucan and [1,6] beta-glucan) linkages present in smaller amounts. The bioactive protein-bound polysaccharides are found in both the fruiting body and in the mycelium.

Biological Activity

Like other mushroom extracts, *Coriolus* requires a hot-water extraction process to pull the polysaccharides out of the indigestible cell walls. The beta-glucans act as "biological response modifiers" in that they activate many components of the immune system. It has been shown that these beta-glucans pass through the gut wall unchanged and into the bloodstream. Receptors for these beta-glucans have been found on neutrophils, monocytes/macrophages, natural killer cells, and also T and B lymphocytes. Recent American research has also demonstrated significant immuno-modulating activity. These unique polysaccharides have been shown to act as potent inducers of proliferation, tumor cytotoxicity, and lymphokine production by human lymphocytes via in vitro studies.

Clinical Studies

Both PSK and PSP are routinely prescribed in Japan and China to stimulate immune function for people who have had surgical treatment for cancer. It is also widely used for immune support for those undergoing chemotherapy or radiation. It is most commonly prescribed for those undergoing treatment for esophageal, lung, stomach, colon, and breast cancer.

Nonsmall Cell Lung Cancer Stages I–III

In a ten-year study researchers examined the effectiveness of *Coriolus* polysaccharides (PSK) in protecting and promoting immune function in 185 people with lung cancer receiving radiation. The study found that "as a result of administering PSK as adjuvant treatment to patients with epidermoid carcinoma of the lung showing satisfactory tumor shrinkage after radiotherapy, the five-year survival rate of the patients with stages I or II disease, as well as stage III, was 39 percent and 22 percent respectively, compared with the nonadministered group's 16 percent and 5 percent. These differences are statistically significant." In addition, patients aged seventy or older who received the combination of PSK and radiation had a significantly higher survival rate than those who only received radiation.

Coriolus Enhances Disease-Free Period after Colon-Cancer Surgery

A ten-year, randomized, double-blind trial was performed by administering *Coriolus* (PSK) to fifty-six patients and a placebo to another group of fifty-five patients after surgical operations on their colorectal cancers. The rate of patients in remission (or disease free) was significantly higher (more than doubled) in the coriolus group as compared to the placebo group. Researchers also found the white blood cells showed "remarkable enhancement in their activities."

Coriolus Polysaccharides Provide Nutritional Support with Chemotherapy

A 1994 study published in the *Lancet* examined the effect of *Coriolus* polysaccharides (PSK) when added to standard chemotherapy with patients who had undergone curative gastrectomy. Two hundred sixty-two patients were randomly assigned standard treatment alone or with *Coriolus* polysaccharides. The minimum follow-up time was five years. The survival rate of the group using the combination of *Coriolus* polysaccharides and chemotherapy was 73 percent after five years. The group receiving chemotherapy alone had a survival rate of 60 percent. Researchers Hiroaki Nakazato et al., concluded that PSK had "a restorative effect in patients who had been immunosuppressed by both recent surgery and subsequent chemotherapy."

Coriolus Alleviates Side Effects of Chemotherapy and Radiation

A study at the Shanghai Teaching University examined whether *Coriolus* polysaccharides (PSP) could lessen the side effects of chemotherapy or radiation. In this study, 650 people with cancer who were undergoing chemotherapy and radiation were given either PSP or a placebo and their side effects assessed. Researchers used twenty different criteria to assess adverse reactions and determined that those receiving PSP had markedly fewer side effects than those receiving placebo.

Supplement Facts

Amount Per Capsule

Coriolus versicolor fruit body extract 20% Beta Glucan (polysaccharide)	400 mg*

*Daily Value not established

Minimum potency to look for in *Coriolus versicolor.*

Known active constituents: protein-bound polysaccharides (beta-1,4-glucan as the main chain with beta-1,3 glucan and beta-1,6 linkages and amino acids)

Clinical Use: Adjunctive treatment for esophageal, lung, stomach, breast, and colon cancer. Used to prevent side effects and immune suppression from chemotherapy and radiation treatments. Used for infections (of the respiratory, urinary, and digestive tracts), hepatitis B and other liver ailments, HIV, general immune weakness, and ringworm.

Dosage: 1,000–4,000 milligrams daily of a hot-water extract containing a minimum of 20–36% polysaccharide (beta-glucan). Take one to four 400-mg capsules twice daily, morning and evening, on an empty stomach.

Safety Profile: Regarded as extremely safe. As an immune modulator it should be used with extreme care or avoided in organ transplant patients using immunosuppressive agents.

5

Maitake

Maitake is one of the best studied mushroom extracts. Indigenous to Northern Japan, maitake has a long history as a valued mushroom, both as a food and as a medicine. Maitake is translated in Japanese as "dancing mushroom." Historical accounts explain the origin of the name, as people would dance with joy when they found maitake because it was so valuable and costly or because maitake is so delicious and healthful. Another explanation is that the fruiting bodies of clustered maitake overlap one another and resemble butterflies in a wild dance.

The Japanese have long used maitake as an adaptogen, a nutrient that helps to balance the various systems and functions of the body.

Evolution of Maitake

In the early 1980s, Dr. Hiroaki Nanba, a professor of microbiology and an expert mycologist at Kobe Pharmaceutical University, was intensively studying the medicinal properties of various mushrooms. During this time, much of his attention was devoted to the popular shiitake mushroom. However, his research showed him that maitake had a unique molecular structure that exhibited greater antitumor activity than other mushroom extracts he had been working with. Maitake, he discovered, also was unique when given orally. In 1984, Dr. Nanba discovered an important maitake fraction (or specialized component) that stimulated macrophages. Through a special extraction method, these maitake fractions were isolated. It was now possible to produce a standardized form of specific beta-glucan polysac-charides—beta-1,6 glucan and beta-1,3 glucan. Later in his re-search, Dr. Nanba patented what is known as MaitakeGold 404®.

According to studies, maitake fractions have the ability to both directly enhance the damaging activity of NK cells against cancer cells and to change NK precursor cells into activated NK cells.

Immune Properties of Maitake

Dr. Nanba and other researchers have identified several mecha-nisms through which maitake beta-glucans provide immune support. Several Japanese studies have been published regard-ing the immuno-modulating effects of maitake.

In 1998, researchers at the University of Massachusetts at Amherst found that an extract of maitake had significant in-hibitory activity against human cervical cancer and T4 leukemic cells. The researchers concluded that further studies were defi-nitely warranted.

Reduces Chemotherapy Side Effects

Maitake is becoming popular to help reduce the side effects of chemotherapy. A survey of 671 patients showed that combining chemotherapy with maitake treatment can reduce adverse reac-tions (such as hair loss, pain, and nausea) as well as diminish the pain that comes with terminal stage cancer.

Maitake also appears to make chemotherapy more effective. One study compared the effects of maitake beta-glucan extract and the chemotherapy drug mitomycin (MMC) on mice with cancer. The maitake beta-glucan alone inhibited tumor growth more effectively (80 percent) than MMC alone (45 percent). How-ever, the most effective tumor inhibition was observed with the combination of these two substances with almost 98 percent inhi-bition. This is an interesting partnership as maitake supports immune function while the MMC directly kills tumor cells.

Cancer Study

A total of thirty-three cancer patients in stages II, III, and IV, ages thirty-three to sixty-eight, participated in this trial. Data was collected under the cooperation of their medical doctors in Japan. Patients were given either maitake beta-glucan with tablets only, or maitake beta-glucan and tablets in addition to chemotherapy. Cancer regression or significant symptom improvement was observed in eleven out of sixteen breast cancer patients, seven out of twelve liver cancer patients, and five out of eight lung cancer patients.

Maitake appears to be most effective against breast, prostate, and liver cancers. To date, it has been less effective against bone, blood, and brain cancers.

Supplement Facts

Amount Per Capsule

Grifola frondosa (Maitake) fruit body extract   400 mg*
20% Beta Glucan (polysaccharide)

*Daily Value not established

Minimum potency to look for in maitake.

Known active constituents: beta-1,3 glucan and beta-1,6 glucan

Clinical Use: Adjunctive cancer treatment, fatigue, high blood pressure, liver disease, and HIV, antioxidant.

Dosage: 300–2,400 mg of a hot-water extract daily, containing a minimum of 20% polysaccharide (beta-glucan). Take one to four capsules twice daily, morning and evening, on an empty stomach. Maitake fractions dosage: for immune support, take 0.5 to 1 milligram of MaitakeGold 404 per kilogram (2.2 pounds) of body weight per day.

Safety Profile: Extremely safe. As an immune modulator it should be used with extreme care or avoided in organ transplant patients using immunosuppressive agents.

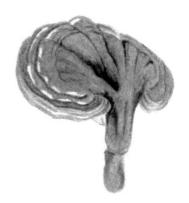

6

Reishi

The reishi mushroom (*Ganoderma lucidum*) is one of the most revered herbs in traditional Chinese and Japanese medicine, with a documented history of over 2,000 years. Known as Ling Zhi in China, there are references to its use in that country as far back as 100 B.C. where it was referred to as the "Herb of Spiritual Potency" and the "Ten-Thousand-Year Mushroom."

Reishi is one of the most highly regarded medicinal mushrooms and is probably the best choice when looking for a general health tonic to improve overall health and increase longevity. It is considered an adaptogen.

Modern clinical research also supports many of the uses for this mushroom as described in traditional medicine. It benefits immune health, cardiovascular health, and liver function. Reishi is also frequently used by mountain climbers to combat altitude sickness and is contained in many of the performance-enhancing herbal formulas used by Chinese athletes.

The fruiting bodies of reishi range from a reddish-orange to an almost black color. The fruiting body also has a shiny look to it (*lucidum* translates to "shiny"). Reishi is extremely difficult to find in the wild but is successfully cultivated for commercial purposes.

Research has demonstrated that reishi has several different active constituents. One group of active constituents is the polysaccharides. The various types of polysaccharides found in reishi have demonstrated immune-enhancing properties. This includes enhancement of several important interleukins.

Another major class of compounds is the triterpenes. These compounds have been reported to have adaptogenic, anti-hypertensive, and anti-allergy effects. Many of the important triterpenes are found only in the mushroom. They are extracted from the shiny red surface of the mushroom, a physical feature missing in the mycelium.

Cardiovascular Benefits

Reishi has been shown in some studies to inhibit platelet aggregation and reduce blood pressure. In one study of thirty-three people with hypertension researchers found blood pressure was significantly reduced over two-weeks' time with reishi supplementation.

Reishi is currently being used in Chinese medicine for the treatment of hypercholesterolemia. It appears to reduce cholesterol via two mechanisms. One is the inhibition of endogenous cholesterol synthesis by inhibiting HMG-CoA Reductase and by inhibiting cholesterol absorption from food sources.

Immune Benefits

Reishi is commonly prescribed by practitioners for long-term immune system support. This includes its use as an adjunctive therapy for cancer. For example, in one placebo-controlled study, forty-eight patients with advanced tumors were given reishi mushroom extract for thirty days. Researchers found a marked immune-modulating effect as demonstrated by an increase in T lymphocytes and decreased CD8 counts. Patients also reported reduced side effects due to chemotherapy or radiation as well as postoperation recovery.

Several studies have demonstrated antitumor activity in animals. More studies are required to confirm this activity in humans.

Studies in China have demonstrated a substantial improvement for patients with chronic bronchitis. In a study of over 2,000 patients with chronic bronchitis there was a 60 to 90 percent improvement within two weeks after beginning a reishi syrup.

Blood Sugar Balance

Animal and in vitro studies have shown reishi to have a blood sugar lowering effect. Much of this activity appears to be due to polysaccharides known as Ganoderans A, B, and C.

It appears there are three main mechanisms behind this hypoglycemic effect. This includes Reishi's ability to elevate plasma insulin levels, to enhance peripheral tissue utilization of glucose, and to enhance liver metabolism of glucose.

Anti-inflammatory Effects

Various animal and in vitro studies have shown that hot-water/ethanol extracts of reishi have anti-inflammatory effects. One study found that 220 milligrams of reishi extract and 50 milligrams of reishi powder had comparable effects to 5 milligrams of hydrocortisone.

Liver Protector

Reishi is commonly used for its hepatoprotective (liver protective) action. One small study of four patients with hepatitis B and elevated liver enzymes (SGOT/SGPT) and bilirubin were given 6 grams of reishi for three months. Significant reduction in SGOT and SGPT were noticed within one month. After three months all values were within normal range.

Altitude Sickness

One of the unique uses of reishi is for altitude sickness. Reishi appears to reduce altitude sickness by oxygenating the blood. This benefit was studied in Chinese mountain climbers that ascended mountains as high as 17,000 feet with minimal reaction. Daily use of reishi should be started ten to fourteen days before you climb the mountain.

Known active constituents: polysaccharides, triterpenes (Ganoderic acids), ergosterols

Clinical Use: Daily tonic to improve and maintain good health, long-term immune support, hepatitis C, hypercholesterolemia, altitude sickness, and diabetes.

Supplement Facts

Amount Per Capsule

Ganoderma lucidum (Red Reishi), fruit body   400 mg*
extract, 10% Beta Glucan (polysaccharide),
4% Triterpenes (ganoderic acids)

---

*Daily Value not established

Minimum potency to look for in reishi.

Dosage: 800 to 4,000 milligrams per day of a hot-water/ethanol extract, containing a minimum of 10% polysaccharide (beta-glucan) and 4% triterpene. Take one to five 400-mg capsules twice daily, morning and evening, on an empty stomach.

Decoction: 375 milliliters twice daily

Safety Profile: No toxicity reported. Occasional digestive upset or skin rash in sensitive users. Caution is advised for those currently using blood-thinning medications due to reishi's anticoagulant effects. Also, caution is advised for those taking hypoglycemic medication due to reishi's potential hypoglycemic activity. As an immune modulator it should be used with extreme care or avoided in organ transplant patients using immunosuppressive agents.

Shiitake

Shiitake (*Lentinula Edodes*) is regarded as a gourmet food in the West, while in Japan and China shiitake is known to be a valuable food and medicinal agent. Its name comes from the Japanese chestnut tree, *shiia,* and the Japanese word for mushroom, *take.* It is also referred to as the "fragrant mushroom" or the "forest mushroom."

This mushroom is indigenous to Japan, China, and other areas of Asia. It is not found in the wild in America but is cultivated for commercial use. Shiitake is the second most common edible mushroom in the world. The fungi is found on dead and injured hardwood trees, including the chestnut tree, hence the prefix *shiia.* Shiitake has a medicinal history of more than 1,000 years and was revered by Japanese emperors. It has been used in traditional Chinese medicine to treat colds, flu, and cardiovascular disease.

Shiitake is used medicinally in two forms in Asia and around the world. This includes lentinan, a purified polysaccharide extracted from the cell wall of the Shiitake fruiting body. The second extract is known as Lentinula edodes mycelium extract, better known as LEM. Both extracts have been shown to enhance immune activity. Both forms have been shown to have a beneficial effect orally but the majority of published data on lentinan has been with the injectable or intravenous forms.

Adjuvant Cancer Therapy

As with many of the medicinal mushrooms, Shiitake has been shown to be of benefit as an adjuvant cancer therapy. It has been shown to improve specific immune markers (including natural killer cells, tumor necrosis factor, T-helper cells, and a variety of interleukins), and patient outcomes. For example, in a study of sixteen people with advanced cancer, lentinan was injected into areas of malignancy. Researchers found that 80 percent of the lesions showed a clinical response, and the survival time for those patients who responded was 129 days and 49 days for those who did not respond.

In a randomized, controlled trial, 275 people with advanced or recurrent stomach cancer were given either chemotherapy and lentinan injections or chemotherapy alone. Using a variety of parameters for analysis, researchers found that the best results occurred when lentinan was given prior to chemotherapy.

Infections

Shiitake extracts have demonstrated a wide variety of activity against various microbes. This includes bacteria (including *Mycobacterium tuberculosis*), parasites, and viruses (including HIV and hepatitis B). More human data is needed to corroborate these initial findings, which were mainly from animal studies.

Cardiovascular Benefits

Current research is demonstrating that shiitake extracts are a promising treatment for high cholesterol levels and for high blood pressure. Human studies have shown that the consumption of high amounts of fresh and dried shiitake resulted in cholesterol decreases that ranged from 7 to 14 percent.

Supplement Facts	
Amount Per Capsule	
Lentinula edodes (Shiitake) extract 10% Beta Glucan (polysaccharide)	400 mg*
*Daily Value not established	

Minimum potency to look for in shiitake.

Known active constituents: polysaccharides with 1-3 beta-D-glucan linkages and a special beta-1,6-D-glucopyranoside branching

Clinical Use: Immune-suppressive diseases such as HIV/AIDS, cancer, colds, flus, candidiasis, high cholesterol, and hepatitis.

Dosage: 800 to 3,000 milligrams of a hot-water extract daily, containing a minimum of 10–20% polysaccharide (beta-glucan). Take one to five capsules twice daily, morning and evening, on an empty stomach.

Safety Profile: Shiitake and the extracts lentinan and LEM are considered nontoxic. There are reports in the literature of rare sensitivity reactions that result in dermatitis.

8

Hericium erinaceus

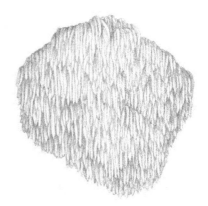

The most recent mushroom extract to excite natural-health enthusiasts is *Hericium erinaceus*. Because it resembles white, icelike pillars, a host of names have arisen to describe it, such as Lion's Mane, Monkey's Head, Monkey's Mushroom, Bear's Head, Old Man's Beard, White Beard, and Hedgehog Mushroom. In Japan it is referred to as Yambushitake and in China it is called Shishigashira. Lion's Mane is found throughout North America, East Asia, and Europe. Besides being used as a medicinal mushroom, Lion's Mane is a choice edible.

Traditional Chinese and Native American Uses

Hericium erinaceus is used in traditional Chinese medicine for the treatment of digestive tract ailments. *H. erinaceus* extract, known as Houtou, is used topically on scratches and cuts to stop bleeding by Native Americans and others.

Immune Properties

H. erinaceus has been the subject of recent studies involving the immune system. As with most of the medicinal mushrooms, unique polysaccharides present in *H. erinaceus* have immune-enhancing properties, and preliminary studies are demonstrating some anticancer effects.

Neurological Properties

The most intriguing potential of *H. erinaceus* is that it may stimulate the production of a substance known as Nerve Growth Factor (NGF). This specialized protein is necessary for the growth of sensory neurons. An in vitro study found that an extract from this mushroom promoted myelin sheath growth on brain cells. The myelin sheath is an important component of neurons that is involved in the transmission of nerve messages. Researchers hope that *H. erinaceus* will prove to be helpful for Alzheimer's disease and other degenerative, neurological conditions. Further studies are needed to clarify whether *H. erinaceus* has any benefit for human neurological conditions.

Supplement Facts

Amount Per Capsule

Hericium erinaceus (Lion's Mane) extract 15% Beta Glucan (polysaccharide)	400 mg*

*Daily Value not established

Minimum potency to look for in *Hericium erinaceus.*

Known active constituents: beta-glucans/polysaccharides, hericenones, erinacines

Safety Profile: No known contraindications or drug interactions.

Clinical Use: Digestive tract ailments, including ulcers and stomach cancer. Cognitive enhancement.

Dosage: 1,000 to 4,000 milligrams of a hot-water extract daily, containing a minimum of 15% polysaccharide (beta-glucan). Take one to five capsules twice daily, morning and evening, on an empty stomach.

9

How to Take Mushroom Supplements

The first step in successfully using mushroom supplements is to understand how to read the label. In general this is best done by reviewing the *Supplement Facts* on the product label. The bottle should clearly state:

1. Mushroom name.

2. Type of extract (look for products that are formulated to the potencies given in the previous mushroom descriptions). This should include the guaranteed percentage and polysaccharide description, unless it is a well-researched isolate, such as MaitakeGold 404.

3. Check with the manufacturer to confirm extraction techniques (hot-water or hot-water/alcohol extracts) as well as quality assurance.

   Hot-water extracted mushroom supplements are usually dehydrated and sold as capsules (except maitake fractions). Hot-water extracts also list the levels of active compounds on the label, making it easy to distinguish them from the other less potent forms of mushroom supplements. Take the recommended dosage between meals for optimal results. If you notice minor digestive upset when taking mushroom extracts on an empty stomach try taking the supplement with food.

Conclusion

There are a variety of medicinal mushrooms that can be used to improve one's health. They represent some of the most effective immune-supportive supplements in the natural foods industry. Historical use and published research has consistently shown that hot-water extracts are the preferred method of extraction for most medicinal mushrooms and mycelium in order to attain therapeutic levels of active constituents. It is also important to select the mushroom extract that is most highly recommended for a particular condition for optimal benefits.

SUMMARY OF MEDICINAL MUSHROOM USES

Agaricus = antitumor

Cordyceps = lung, kidneys, adrenals, energy, libido, asthma, bronchitis, and tinnitus

Coriolus = chemotherapy support; lung, colon, liver, breast, and stomach cancer; and HIV

Maitake = breast and prostate cancer, and HIV

Reishi = liver, cholesterol, and daily immune tonic; hepatitis; HIV; anti-inflammatory; antiviral

Shiitake = antimicrobial, cholesterol, immune support

Hericium = stomach and cognitive enhancement

References

Alexopoulos, C. J. and C. W. Mims. *Introductory Mycology*. Wiley, 1979, p. 10.

Aoki,T. 1984. "Lentinan." In *Immune Modulation Agents and Their Mechanisms*, R. L. Fenichel and M. A. Chirgis, eds. *Immunology Studies*. 25:62–77.

Bensky, D., et al. *Materia Medica of Chinese Herbal Medicine*. Eastland Press, Seattle, 1993, pp. 338–39.

Chang, H. M. and P. But. *Pharmacology and Applications of Chinese Materia Medica*. Vol.1. Singapore: World Scientific, 1986.

Chen, D. G. Effects of JinShuiBao capsule on the quality of life of patients with chronic heart failure. *J Administration Traditional Chinese Med* 5(suppl), (1995):40–45.

Chen, Y. P., et al. Comparisons of fermented *Cordyceps mycelia* and natural *Cordyceps sinensis* in treating 30 patients with renal failure. *Chinese Traditional Herbal Drugs* 17(6), (1986):256–258.

Cheng, Z., et al. Effects of ling zhi on hemorrheology parameters and symptoms of hypertension patients with hyperlipidemia and sequelae of cerebral thrombosis. In: Shu S. and M. Mori, eds., *The Research on* Ganoderma lucidum (*Part One*). Volume 1. Shanghai Med Univ., 1993, pp. 339–342.

Cheng, J. H., et al. Analysis of therapeutic effect of Jinshuibao capsule in adjuvant treatment of 20 patients with terminal stage of lung cancer. *J Administration Traditional Chinese Med* 5(suppl), (1995): 34–35.

Chihara, G., et al. Inhibition of mouse sarcoma 180 by polysaccharides from *Lentinus edodes* (Shiitake). *Nature*, 222 (1969): 637.

Feng, M. G., et al. Vascular dilation by fermented mycelia of *Cordyceps sinensis* in anesthetized dogs. *J Chinese Materia Medica* 12(12), (1987):745–749.

Fujimaya, Y., et al. Tumor specific cytocidal and immunopotentiating effects of relatively low molecular weight products derived from the basidiomycete, *Agaricus blazei* Murill. *Anticancer Res*, 19 (1999):113–118.

Fujimiya, Y., et al. Selective tumoricidal effect of soluble proteglucan extracted from the basidiomycete, Agaricus blazei Murill, mediated via natural killer cell activation and apoptosis. Cancer Immunol Immunother, 46 (1998):147–159.

Hans, SR. Experiences in treating patients of chronic bronchitis and pulmonary diseases with Cs-4 capsule (JinShuiBao). *J. Administration Traditional Chinese Med* 5(suppl), (1995): 33–34.

Hayakawa, K., N. Mitsuhashi, and Y. Saito, et al. Effect of krestin (PSK) as adjuvant treatment on the prognosis after radical radiotherapy in patients with non-small cell lung cancer. *Anticancer Res.*, 13(5C): September–October, (1993): 1815–1820.

He, X. G., Seleen, J., Chemical Analysis as Quality Control Method for Medicinal Mushroom Extracts, *International Journal of Medicinal Mushrooms*, 6(3), (2004) 253–261.

Hikino, H., et al. Mechanisms of hypoglycemic activity of ganodernan B: A glycan of *Ganoderma lucidum* fruit bodies. *Planta Med* 55(4), (1989):385.

Hiroaki, Nakazato, et al. Efficacy of immunochemotherapy as adjuvant treatment after curative resection of gastric cancer. *Lancet* vol. 343 (1994).

Hobbs, C. *Medicinal Mushrooms*. Loveland, CO: Interweave Press Inc., 1996, p.110.

Huang, Y., et al. Toxicity study of fermentation *Cordyceps mycelia* B1414. Zhongchengyao Yanjiu (10), (1987): 24–25.

Ikuzawa, M., et al. Fate and Distribution of an Anti-Tumor Protein-Bound Polysaccharide PSK (Krestin). *International Journal of Immunopharmacology* 10(4), (1988): 415–423.

Ito, H., et al. Anti-tumor effects of a new polysaccharide-protein complex (ATOM) prepared from *Agaricus blazei* (Iwade strain 101) and its mechanisms in tumor-bearing mice. *Anticancer Res.*, 17 (1997): 277–284.

Jong, S. C. and J. M. Birmingham. Medicinal benefits of the mushroom *Ganoderma*. *Adv Appl Microbiol* 37 (1992):101–134.

Kolotushkina, E. V., M. G. Moldavan, and K. Y. Voronin, et al. The influence of *Hericium erinaceus* extract on myelination process in vitro. *Fiziol Zh* 49(1), 2003: 38–45.

Kupin, V. A new biological response modifier *Ganoderma lucidum* and its application in oncology. In: Proceedings of the 4th international symposium on *Ganoderma lucidum;* Seoul. Cancer Res Ctr, June 10, 1992, pp.49–50.

Liu, B., and Y. Bau. *Fungi Pharmacopoeia*. Kiniko Press, 1980, pp. 170–172.

Lou, Y., et al. Cardiovascular pharmacological studies of ethanol extracts of *Cordyceps mycelia* and *Cordyceps* fermentation solution. *Chinese Traditional and Herbal Drugs* 17(5), (1986):17–21; 209–213.

Lovy, A., B. Knowles, and R. Labbe, et al. Activity of edible mushrooms against the growth of human T4 leukemic cancer cells, HeLa cervical cancer cells, and Plasmodium falciparum. *Journal of Herbs, Spices, and Medicinal Plants* 6(4), (1998): 49–57.

Manabe, N., et al. Effects of the mycelial extract of cultured *Cordyceps sinensis* on in vivo hepatic energy metabolism in the mouse. *Jpa J Pharmacol* (1), (1996):85–88.

Mizuno, M., et al. Polysaccharides from *Agaricus blazei* stimulate lymphocyte T cell subsets in mice. *Biosoci Biotechnol Biochem.* 62 (1998):434–437.

Morikawa, K., R. Takeda, M.Yamazaki, et al. Induction of tumoricidal activity of polymorphonuclear leukocytes by a linear 1,3-D-glucan and other immuno-modulators in murine cells. *Cancer Res.* 45: (1985): 1496–1501.

Nakazato H., A. Koike, and S. Saji, et al. Efficacy of immunochemotherapy as adjuvant treatment after curative resection of gastric cancer. Study Group of Immunochemotherapy with PSK for Gastric Cancer. *Lancet* 7;343(8906), (May 1994):1122–1126.

Nanba, H. Maitake D fraction: Healing and preventive potential for cancer. *J Orthomol Med* 12(1), 1997: 43–49.

———. *Maitake Challenges Cancer.* Kobe, Japan: Socio Health Group, 1998.

———. Presented at the 3rd International Conference on Mushroom Biology and Mushroom Products in Sydney, Australia (October 1999).

Nanba, H. and P. Kumar. *The Therapeutics of Maitake Mushroom in Japan.* Kobe, Japan: New Editions Health World, 1995, p. 21.

Oka, M., et al. Immunological analysis and clinical effects of intrabdominal and intrapleural injection of lentinan for malignant ascites and pleural effusion. *Biotherapy* 5 (1992):107–112.

Shao, G., et al. Treatment of hyperlipidemia with *Cordyceps sinensis:* A double blind placebo control trial. *Intl J Orient Med* 15(2), (1990): 77–80.

Shiao, M. S., et al. Natural products and biological activities of the Chinese medicinal fungus *Ganoderma lucidum. Am Chem Soc* 547 (1994):342–354.

Soo, T. S. The therapeutic value of *Ganoderma lucidum.* In Buchanan et al., *Ganoderma systematics, phytopathology and pharmacology.* Proceedings of contributed symposium 59A, B; 5th International Mycological Congress; Vancouver (August 14–21, 1994), pp.105–113.

Stavinhoa, W. B., et al. Study of the anti-inflammatory activity of *Ganoderma lucidum.* Research paper presented at the Third Academic/Industry Joint Conference; August 18–20, 1990; Sapporo Park Hotel (Japan).

Sun, Z., et al. The ameliorative effect of PSP on the toxic and side reaction of chemo and radiotherapy of cancers. In *Advanced Research in PSP,* Q. Yang, ed.

Hong Kong: Hong Kong Association for Health Care Ltd., 1999 Suzuki, S. and S. Ohshima. Influence of Shi-Ta-Ke (*Lentinus edodes*) on human serum cholesterol. *Mushroom Science IX (Part 1)*. Proceedings of the Ninth International Scientific Congress on the Cultivation of Edible Fungi, Tokyo (1974): 463–467.

Taguchi, T., et al. 1982. Clinical Trials on Lentinan (Polysaccharide). In Yamamura, Y., et al. (eds.) *Immunomodulation by Microbial Products and Related Synthetic Compounds*. New York: Elsevier Science Publishing Company, pp. 467–475.

Tomada, M., et al. Glycan structures of ganoderans B and C, hypoglycemic glycans of *Ganoderma lucidum* fruit bodies. *Phytochemistry* 25:28 (1988):17–20.

Torisu, M., Y. Hayashi and T. Ishimitsu, et al. Significant prolongation of disease-free period gained by oral polysaccharide K (PSK) administration after curative surgical operation of colorectal cancer. *Cancer Immunol Immunother* 31(5), (1990):261–268.

Torisu, M., et al. Significant prolongation of disease-free period gained by oral PSK (*Coriolus* versicolor) administration after curative surgical operation of colon cancer. *Cancer Immunology Immunotherapy* 31 (1990):261–268.

Upton, R., et al. Reishi Mushroom (*Ganoderma lucidum*) Standards of Analysis, Quality Control, and Therapeutics. *American Herbal Pharmacopoeia* (September 2000), p. 9.

Wang, J.C., S. H. Hu, C. H. Su, et al. Antitumor and immunoenhancing activities of polysaccharide from culture broth of *Hericium* spp. *Fiziol Zh* 49(1), (2003):38–45.

Xie, Z., et al. *Dictionary of Traditional Chinese Medicine*. The Commercial Press Ltd., Hong Kong, (1988), p. 201.

Xu, J. M. and H. J. Zheng. Treating 64 patients with arrhythmia by Ningxinbao capsule: A randomized, double-blind observation. *Shanghia J Traditional Chinese Med* (4):4–5:1994.

Yang, W., et al. Clinical study of fermentation product of *Cordyceps sinensis* on treatment of hyposexuality. *J Admin Traditional Chinese Med* 5(suppl) (1995):23–24.

Zhang, Z., et al. Clinical and laboratory studies of JinShuiBao in cavenging oxygen free radicals in elderly senescent XuZheng patients. *J Admin Traditional Chinese Med* 5 (suppl) 1995:14–18.

Zhou, L. T., et al. Short term curative effect of cultured *Cordyceps sinensis* (Berk) Sacc. Mycelia in chronic hepatitis B. *China J Chinese Materia Medica* 15(1) (1990): 14–18;53–55.

Index

About the Author

Mark Stengler, N.D., is a leading naturopathic doctor and author of more than sixteen books on natural healing. These include the best-selling *The Natural Physician's Healing Therapies and Prescription for Natural Cures*. He is a frequent guest on national television and radio shows. Dr. Stengler served on a committee for the Yale University Complementary Medicine Outcomes Research Project. He is in private practice in La Jolla, California. His website is www.lajollawholehealth.com.

THE REAL FACTS ABOUT
ETHIOPIA

by

J. A. ROGERS

Author of

"From Superman To Man,"
"World's Greatest Men and Women of African Descent," etc.

9781639233700

Printed August, 2021

Cover Art By: Paul Amid

Published and Distributed By:
Lushena Books
607 Country Club Drive, Unit E
Bensenville, IL 60106
www.lushenabks.com

ISBN: 9781639233700

Editor's Note

The Real Facts About Ethiopia was first written and published by J.A. Rogers in 1936. The 1982 edition was reprinted from a copy in the Special Collection of The Atlanta University Center, Robert W. Woodruff Library. We would like to thank the Special Collection Librarian, Ms. Gloria Mims for her assistance in making this copy available.

FOREWORD

"The chief danger to the white man arises from his arrogant contempt for other races, a contempt which in America is mixed with fear and hate and which has provoked fear and hatred in return. Europeans have recently enjoyed a fair advantage over their rivals which they have abused without the slightest regard for justice and fair play. This advantage will not be theirs in the future."—Dean Inge (The White Man and his Rivals.)

"You are forcing on the world the coming struggle between Asia, all Asia against Europe and America . . . You are heaping up material for . . . a gigantic Day of Reckoning . . . You are deaf to the voice of reason and fairness and so you will be taught with the whirling swish of the sword when it is red."—Achmed Abdullah.

For the past four centuries the European, or white race, has been colonizing in all the lands of the darker races. Thanks to its superior developments in death-dealing implements and the marked difference in the color of its skin it was enabled to set itself off as a superior race and to indulge in a orgy of plunder, murder, and extermination. This happening in the very lands of the colored peoples wounded their pride, aroused their deepest hate, and created in the hearts of darker peoples, totally unknown to one another, a common hostility to white peoples.

For centuries this animosity slumbered like a volcano, bursting at times into revenge as in the attacks on missionaries; the Indian Mutiny; or the Zulu uprising. Then two events came to arouse a unifying consciousness —black Ethiopia's defeat of white Italy in 1896, and colored Japan's victory over white Russia in 1905.

The growing resentment of the darker races against white supremacy stirred the far-seeing thinkers. White writers, hostile to the darker peoples as Putnam Weale, J. W. Gregory, Lothrop Stoddard, and Maurice Muret, and others friendly to them as Sir Harry Johnston, Jean Finot, Dean Inge and Sir Leo Money saw a conflict and even a war between the races. Colored writers as Achmed Abdullah of Afghanistan and W. E. B. Du-Bois of America have foreseen the same.

Whether this prediction will come true remains to be seen. But in this threat of Italy against Ethiopia another and very definite stage of colored opposition to white injustice has been reached. In this unjustified aggression against the last stronghold of black civilization the darker peoples of the world see a challenge to their very existence.

These darker races outnumber the white four to one. Two of the three foremost nations of the world, Britain and France, are almost wholly dependent upon the co-operation of their colored subjects. Of the 500,000,-000 people in the British Empire, 430,000,000 are colored. In the French empire 125,000,000 of the 170,000,000 are.

Of the 160,000,000 inhabitants of Africa, less than 3,000,000 are white. The sentiment of the white, or near-white North African, is anti-white and distinctly African. The blacks of Africa outnumber the whites 60 to 1, and in some sections a hundred to one.

From the poison of this universal color-line Britain will suffer the worst effect. This seems only just as she has been the first, the chief, and the strongest builder of the color-line. So firmly did Britain lay the foundations of this evil in the American colonies that centuries later it still defies all attacks of intelligence, commonsense, and humanity. So thoroughly did Britain teach her offspring, the United States, the lesson of racial discrimination and exploitation that the United States with her lynchings and burnings-alive of black people, was, prior to Mussolini's threat against Ethiopia, the foremost agent in keeping alive the resentment of the colored races against the white—the foremost in keeping open the old wounds of race hate.

A war in Africa, whichever way it goes, will be disastrous to Britain. If Ethiopia wins it will stir the pride of the African and urge him to oust the whites; if Ethiopia loses it will stir revenge and the effect will be the same. The 320,000,000 dark-skinned people of India will be similarly affected, now or later.

Whatever be the outcome of the threatened Italian aggression against Ethiopia the world consciousness of the darker races against white exploitation has been intensified and will not subside. As General Hertzog has said it seems that a deeper and more cruel era of hate, ill-will, and war than the world has even known is about to begin. The avalanche is on its way and it will not stop until the last vestiges of the brutal and debasing color-line imposed on the world by the white race shall have been shattered into irretrievable fragments.

One hears much about a union of English-speaking peoples to ensure world peace and brotherhood. The first step towards any such goal would have to be a union of Britain and America to wipe out their cruel color-line. Unless they do this, there will never be any peace until they meet the inevitable end of the unjust and oppressive nations.

We want no more wars, economic or racial. End color discrimination.

Gregory, J. W. Menace of Color. Phila., 1925.

Inge, Dean. Quar. Review. April, 1921.

Stoddard, Lothrop. Rising Tide of Color Against White World Supremacy. N. Y., 1920.

DuBois, W. E. B. Darkwater. N. Y., 1920.

Maurice Muret. Twilight of the White Races., N. Y., 1926.

Money, Sir Leo. The Peril of the White. London, 1925.

Spengler, O. The Decline of the West.

Abdullah, Achmed. Forum, Vol. 52, p. 484-497.

Ellis, W. Inviting a War of the Races. Overland Monthly.

Finot, Jean. Race Prejudice.

OF WHAT RACE ARE THE ETHIOPIANS ?

ECAUSE of the increasing importance of the Ethiopians in world affairs, certain writers, inspired no doubt by their old prejudice against the Aframericans, are widely denying that there is any racial relationship whatever between Ethiopian and Aframerican. The Ethiopians, according to these writers, are "Semitic," "Hamitic," "Caucasian," "without a single drop of Negro blood," etc., etc.

Now as regards the word "Negro" there are two interpretations, which are widely different, namely, the American and the universal. In the United States one as fair as a Scandinavian may be socially and legally a "Negro." Further, a black man who speaks with a foreign accent, wears a turban, or is of another nationality may be told that he is not a "Negro." For instance, there was the case of Dr. Hubert Harrison, a distinguished native of the Virgin Islands. Dr. Harrison was a full-blooded Negro if ever there was one. When, however, he applied for naturalization papers, he was set down by the authorities as "White." Harrison was Danish and in the ethnological omniscience of the State Department Danes are white, hence Harrison though coal-black was a white man. This writer saw the papers. The same was true of another light-colored Negro from Jamaica,

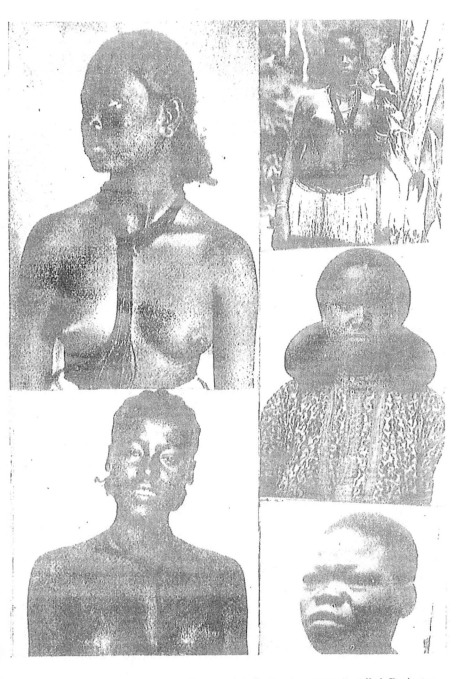

Some of the Ethiopian racial types. Lowest right is the type that is called Baria or Negro, in Ethiopia and the Near East. (Photo by the Author).

West Indies, whose papers were filled in thus: "Color, white; complexion, brown." Negro Porto Ricans are also set down as White.

In short, "Negro" in the United States is sometimes caste, sometimes race, sometimes both. Really to be able to define what is a Negro a scrambled brain is the first essential. And a touch of lunacy qualifies one as an expert.

In other lands, however, a Negro is usually an unmixed black man with wooly hair, thick lips, etc.

In the Orient, on the other hand, one drop of high-caste "blood" makes one high caste. It is culture, not color that counts. Africans, who come from the interior are of cruder culture and are looked down on much, as in our lands, country-folks are. But from the days of the Pharaohs Negroes - from the interior who had the ability and the power, suffered little handicap. Many rose even to be rulers, one of the most conspicuous examples being Kafur.

"White" and "Negro," it must be remembered, are English. Their application to peoples of native African and Arabian descent is, therefore, an attempt by the English-speaking to denote social status. But since Orientals think not so much in terms of race as in terms of the social standing of the individual and that also of his tribe or nationality, color designations as "White" and "Negro" are almost meaningless to them. In Cairo, Egypt, the writer once saw a man of the deepest shade of ebony, with short, wooly hair and a Grecian nose. A dragoman, or guide, who was about three-fourths Negro, and was a Bedouin, told him that the man was a Negro; that his parents held others like him as slaves in Arabia, and that he, himself was not a Negro. Others, when questioned, confirmed this. Tippoo Tip, first ruler of the Belgian Congo, for instance, was known as an Arab, that is, a White man, but to all appearances, he was a full-blooded Negro. Much the same is true in Latin-American countries especially Brazil, where even dark mulattoes are classed as White. In short, in the Orient and Latin America wealth and social position, not color or hair, often determines "race."

In this sense then certain Ethiopian peoples as the Somali, Amharas, Tigreans, Shoans, who show some White admixture, would not be Negroes; only those like the Chankalla and the Yumbos, who show none would be.

If, however, we use the American definition of Negro, which includes all the shades from black to light-yellow and white, and all textures of hair from silky blond to tightly-curled wool, then every Ethiopian this writer has ever seen would be a "Negro" and nearer to the "pure" type than the average Aframerican.

The writer affirms this after having observed the Negroid type for thirty years in all its manifestations, and after having seen Negroes of nearly every nationality on the five continents—French, American, English, Portuguese, German, Australian, Egyptian, Sudanese, Haitian, Brazilian, Arabian, West Indian, etc., etc.

Some Somalis have straight black hair, but so have many Aframericans of Indian descent. Besides the Somalis would be uniformly darker. In short, even in the most learned and scientific circles there has never been any agreement as to what is a Negro. Writers like Elliot-Smith, Lady Lugard, and Dr. Junker have their definition of Negro; others equally informed as Sir Harry Johnston, Jean Finot, and Prof Dorsey, theirs, also.

As for Hamitic that is only a dark mulatto type which has become fixed by inter-breeding. A "son of Ham" has always been supposed to be a black man. It would be easy to pick out any number of what the scientists call Hamitic from among the mulattoes of the United States and

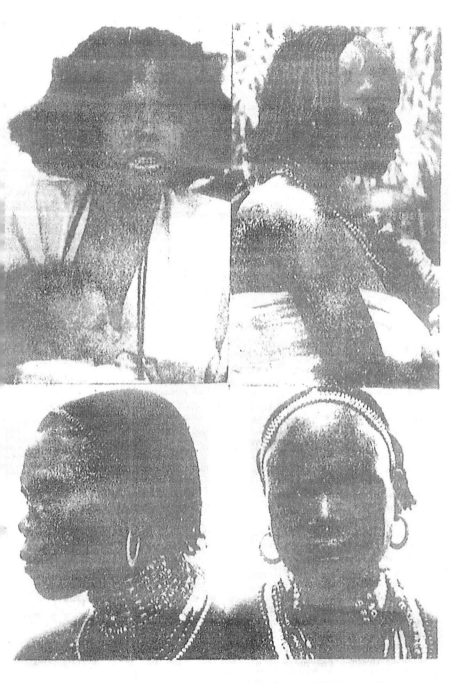

Above: Two Ethiopian mothers. Below: Two Ethiopian belles.

the West Indies. This was the type that seemed to have predominated in Ancient Egypt and still does in modern one.

In reality there are only two varieties of mankind, the black and the white. All the others, as the Mongolian and the Indian, are in between. This is a commonsense view. But in ethnology, as in phrenology and theology, there is need for a mass of mystifying names in order to impress the uninformed.

As regards the Asiatic origin of the Ethiopians, it appears that a people known as the Habesha, migrated to Ethiopia from Yemen, Arabia. Some writers are insisting therefore that the Ethiopians are Asiatics. But that was before the Christian era. White people have been living in the New World only five centuries. Does one still call the descendants of Europeans in America, European?

Further the Yemenites are not only Negroid but it appears that all the present inhabitants of Africa, save the pigmies, originated in Asia.

As for the Semitic origin, there was a considerable migration of Jews to Ethiopia with Menelik I. But that was in 955 B. C. For the past 2,800 years these Semites have been mixing with the African natives until in some cases they are indistinguishable from them. Besides there was considerable Negro strain in the Jews in Solomon's time. Again the Falashas, a people of Jewish origin, still live in Ethiopia. They are black and unmistakably Negroid. Semitic, indicates language, not race. A Semite like an English-speaking person may be black or white.

Some white strain came into Ethiopia with the Portuguese and some has filtered in from Egypt, but not much.

The ruling classes of Ethiopians have mixed freely with the purer type Negroes. The masters have had children by these Negro women, and since there is no racial discrimination in Ethiopia the offspring also entered the ruling classes. Menelik II, the greatest of their rulers after Haile Selassie, was at least seven-eighths Negro.

"The Negro blood dominated in him (Menelik) as it did in many other Ethiopian chiefs" (I. L. Blanchot, Geographie, Dec. 1920, p. 451).

"Menelik's mother was a woman of low origin * * * giving him the Negroid face" (National Georgraphic Magazine, Vol. XII, p. 94).

As regards Haile Selassie, W. Alexander Powell, an American traveler, tells of a white American woman, who, when she saw him riding in state in Paris with Premier Poincare on the Champs-Elysees and later in the movies being entertained by King George, King Albert, and King Victor Emmanuel, wanted to know why all this fuss was being made "over a common African nigger."

"Yet," adds Powell, "the dusky little man who drove through the Paris streets . . . far from being a Negro is of blood as purely Caucasian as that of the American woman . . . " (Beyond the Utmost Purple Rim, p. 292).

Col. Powell thus sees Haile Selassie as a white man. But let us suppose that instead of being a guest of the Emperor, Powell had seen him riding incognito in a Pullman car or eating in an American restaurant, what would have been his feelings? From the Negrophobic tone of his book it is safe to say that they would have been the same as those of the white woman he rebuked.

Pictures of the Ethiopians that have been appearing in the newsreels and the newspapers fully confirm moreover what has been said of their Negroid strain. The more accurate news writers are doing the same. An Associated Press dispatch says "Hundreds of Ethiopian boys looking like Southern pickaninnies . . . strutted alongside bearded septugenarians who might have stepped from the pages of 'Uncle Tom's Cabin' " (N. Y. Post,

Aug. 21, 1935). In short, Africans are generally Negroid, as Eastern Asiatics are Mongoloid, and Europeans, Caucasoid.

Certain Ethiopian individuals who are eager for "white" culture would no doubt be proud if called white as certain mulattoes in the West Indies and South America would be, but the majority would be just as much displeased as the average white Southerner would be if called a Negro. The principal reason is that they know that the white man, or the red man, as they call him, covets their country.

This difference must be noted however. The Ethiopians have never drawn a color-line against white peoples.

———

For list of authorities on the Negro strain in the Jews, ancient and modern, consult "Jews and Ethiopians" in Rogers, J. A. "100 Amazing Facts About the Negro," with "The Key."

GENERAL HISTORY OF ETHIOPIA

ETHIOPIAN history goes so far into the past that what is said of its beginnings cannot be proved. But neither can it be disproved.

The name of its founder, according to the most reliable records, was Cush. The date of its founding is set at 6280 B. C., which is three times as long as from the birth of Christ to the present time, or a total of 8,200 years.

It had two capitals, Napata and Meroe, whose mighty ruins still stand. Ethiopia was known to the Egyptians as the land of Ksh (Cush). The word, Ethiopia, like the word, Egypt, is of Greek origin and came into use much later. The Egyptians called their land, Khemi. The Ethiopians probably called themselves Nubians.

This part of Ethiopia is now in the Anglo-Egyptian Sudan.

Another Ethiopia also extended to the south-east on the Red Sea. This was Habashat—the Abaseni (Abyssinia) of the Greeks—and was a part, or a province, of the first. It might even have been its mother-land. This part of Ethiopia was also founded by Cush, and its capital was Axum, whose relics also speak of a mighty past. Later these two Ethiopias seemed to have drifted apart for in the Fourth Century A. D. the Abyssinian Ethiopia invaded the Nubian one.

Ethiopia, in its earliest history included not only Africa but Southern Asia as far as India, according to Herodotus (525-484 B. C.). So-called Negro peoples predominated then in Asia Minor. Nimrod, the mighty hunter, a son of Cush, was founder of the Assyrian Empire. In Southern Arabia, Southern India, Siam, as far as Australia, and the islands of the Pacific, the Negroid type prevailed, and still does. Prof. Dorsey, one of the foremost and most realistic of the modern anthropologists says, "Wherever the Indian Ocean touches land it finds dark-skinned people with stron developed jaws, relatively long arms, and kinky or frizzly hair. Call that the Indian Ocean, or Negroid division of the human race" (Why We Behave Like Human Beings, p. 44.)

Ethiopia was generally believed by the most ancient scholars to have been the first of the nations and the mother of civilization. Modern scholars, basing their opinion on excavations, generally deny this. But since much is yet undiscovered, and since the ancient scholars were nearer the event, it seems logical to give them the benefit of the doubt until such time as the modern scholars have filled the gaps in their records.

Further, it is not unlikely that civilization might have come from the Ethiopians of Asia rather than from those of Africa?

In any case there is at least one proved connection between the two Ethiopias, namely, the written language of modern Ethiopia, or Ghez, is derived from the Meroitic, or ancient Ethiopian.

There can be no doubt as to racial identity of Ethiopians. Their monuments show them to be what we call Negroes today. The Encyldpedia Britannica says of these monuments, "The figures are obese, especially the women, and have the pronounced Negro features, and the royal person is loaded with bulging golden ornaments." Prof. Breasted particularly notes the Negroid features of one of the greatest of the Ethiopian rulers, Taharka, or Tirhaquah of the Bible.

Ethiopia was for a long time dominated by Egypt. But in 721 ˆB. C. her king, Piankhi, conquered Egypt to the mouth of the Nile.

In 712 B. C. Sabacon, son-in-law of Piankhi, established the XXV, or Ethiopian Dynasty in Egypt. Taharka, a nephew of Sabacon, extended Ethiopian mastery in Assyria, and for a time gave her world mastery; but defeated by the Assyrians he retreated up the Nile to the original Ethiopian domains.

In 525 B. C. Cambyses, the Persian king, invaded Ethiopia and was repulsed by Nastasen.

The first king of Abyssinian Ethiopia was Ori, 4470 B. C. Haile Selassie I, is its 334th ruler. Modern Ethiopians have a connected list of their kings since Ori.

Ethiopia has been at war since the days of the Pharaohs. The chief reasons for this were that she owned the sources of the Nile and was rich in gold, which the Egyptians and others were ever striving for. After the Egyptians came the Mohammedans who from the seventh to the nineteenth centuries warred with Ethiopia for the same reason. It is these centuries of war with Islam which is probably the chief cause for the backwardness of Ethiopia among the nations today.

OTHER HIGHLIGHTS OF ETHIOPIAN HISTORY
Nubia or Cushite Ethiopia

1270 B. C. Memmon. King of Ethiopia, left Susa, his capital in Persia, with an army of 200,000 men (half white, and half black) to go to the aid of his uncle, King Priam, in the famous Trojan War.

944 B. C. Zera. King of Ethiopia, invaded Egypt and Palestine with an army of 1,000,000 men (according to the Bible) and is beaten back by disease and the armies of Asa, King of Judea.

30 B. C. The Romans invaded Ethiopia, and destroyed the capital, Napata.

20 B. C. Candace III, ruler of Ethiopia, invaded Egypt and pillaged Thebes.

Habashat, or Sheban, or Abyssinian Ethiopia

981 B. C: Makeda, Queen of Sheba, visited King Solomon in Judea.

955 B. C. Their son, Menelik mounted the throne of Ethiopia.

70 A. D. Juda, the eunuch of Candace, baptised by the Apostle Philip.

70 A. D. Candace established Christianity at her capital, Axum, making Ethiopia the first Christian nation.

341 A. D. Christianity restored in Ethiopia by Abraha and St. Frumentius.

524 A. D. The Ethiopians invaded Arabia and captured Yemen from the Jews.

569. The Ethiopians attacked Mecca and are repulsed. From this event started a world war that lasted more than a thousand years.

601. The Ethiopians were driven back across the Red Sea, later to lose all their coast-line to the Mohammedans.

937. Judith, Queen of the Falashas, or Black Jews, seized the Ethiopian throne and ruled 40 years.

977. Tekla Haimanot, Ethiopian saint, overthrew the Black Jews and restored the dynasty of Solomon and the Queen of Sheba.

1192. King Lalibala built the famous rock temples of Lasta, and invaded Arabia.

1434. King Zara Jacob sent envoys to the Council of Florence, Italy.

1442. Pedro de Covilham, envoy of John II, king of Portugal, visited Eskender II, king of Ethiopia.

1529. The war of centuries between Ethiopia and Islam continued. The terrible Mohammedan general, Mohammed-Gerad, invaded Ethiopia.

1544. The Ethiopians, aided by the Portuguese, routed the Mohammedans and killed Mohammed-Gerad.

1649. King Fasildas drove the Portuguese from Ethiopia.

1843. Sahle-Selassie, "The Great," made a treaty with France.

1867. A British army, 15,000 strong, invaded Ethiopia to free white missionaries.

1889. The Mahdists, 40,000 strong, are repulsed with terrible slaughter by King John. This practically marked the close of 1,100 years of th ? Mohammedan attempt to seize Ethiopia.

1896. Menelik defeated the Italians at Adowa.

1916. Battle of Sagalle. Lidj Yassue, Ethiopian Emperor, beaten by Haile Selassie. 20,000 slain. Zaiditu placed on the throne.

1923. Ethiopia entered the League of Nations.

1930. Haile Selassie crowned Emperor.

1934. Armed conflict for possession of the oasis of Walwal in Ethiopia started the great Italo-Ethiopian quarrel.

BOOKS ON ETHIOPIAN HISTORY

Budge, Sir E. A. W. The History of Ethiopia. 2 vols. London, 1928.
Budge, Sir E. A. W. The Egyptian Sudan. 2 vols. London, 1907.
Reisner, G. A. Excavations at Nuria—The Kings of Ethiopia. Harvard African Studies. II. Varia Africana II.
Reisner, G. A. The Pyramids of Meroe and The Candaces of Ethiopia, in Museum of Fine Arts. Bull. Boston, Mass., April, 1923.
Morie, L. J. Histoire de l'Ethiopie, 2 vols., Paris, 1904.
Sellassie, G. Chronique du Regne de Menelik II. 2 vols, Paris, 1930 (The author is an Ethiopian).
Littman, E. Deutsche Axum-Expedition. 4 vols. Berlin, 1913.
The Catholic Encyclopedia (see Cush) vol. IV. p. 575.
(All but Morie's are illustrated.)
Read also "Abraha Al-Arsham, Emperor of Yemen and Ethiopia" in "World's Greatest Men and Women of African Descent," by J. A. Rogers.
For additional facts and authorities on Ethiopians and their descent see also Rogers, J. A. 100 Amazing Facts About the Negro with "The Key."

THE STORY OF ITALIAN AGGRESSION AGAINST ETHIOPIA

TALY'S dealings with Ethiopia have been marked with trickery and coveteousness from the first. Whenever the Ethiopians out-tricked the Italians, however, and this was often, it was charged to that spirit of treachery, thievery, and craftiness supposed to inhere in African peoples.

Let us review briefly the earlier history of this Italo-Ethiopian strife. It is highly necessary to an understanding of the present quarrel. Let us also remember, at the outset, that the two countries are 4,000 miles apart, and that the only Ethiopians who have ever tried to enter Italy are students, tourists and religious pilgrims.

In 1876, when that arch-murderer, voluptuary, and lover of good things to eat, Leopold II, King of the Belgians, took away the rich empire of the Congo from its owner, Tippoo Tib, an Arab Negro, he started a rush of the European powers that in less than 30 years took away nearly all of Africa from its original owners.

At that time Italy was too exhausted from her long struggle for independence against Austria and the Pope to reach out for any. In 1869 when the Suez Canal was opened, however, the Rubattino Steamship Company, an Italian concern, leased the port of Assab on the Red Sea from the Sultan of Raheita as a coaling station. In March, 1870, Rubattino bought the port outright for $9,440.

Ten years later, the Italian government, spurred by the rich loot being taken out of the so-called Dark Continent by Leopold and others, began to have African aspirations. She recalled the vast empire that Rome once held in Africa. Accordingly, she gave Rubattino $43,200 for Assab and placed it under her flag.

Most of the land along the Red Sea, though worthless for agriculture, is of high strategic value. It lies on the route to India, England's most prized possession. England, therefore, highly mistrustful of the entry of any other power in this region, made strong protest. So did Egypt and Turkey, who owned territory there. It is notable that at this time the only friend that Italy had in East Africa was Ethiopia. Finally, after much negotiation, British objections were overcome, and those of Egypt and Turkey ignored.

On July 5, 1882, Italy formally placed Assab under the Italian crown. This was the first colony she had had in Africa since the days of the Caesars.

With her appetite now whetted, Italy reached out for Massowah, a port with a rich trade with the interior, and Europe and Asia, since the time of Cleopatra. This time England was much more cordial. She was being beaten by the Mahdi, the great Negro prophet of the Soudan, and she welcomed another white power. Hence she permitted Italy to grab Massowah from Egypt. Encouraged, Italy continued to acquire territory along the Red Sea by tactics that are mostly dubious, until she had nearly 40,000 square miles. This she consolidated into the colony of Erithrea—45,374 square miles—in 1890.

While on the subject of Italian expansion in Africa, let us finish with it. Her next acquisition was in Somaliland, where she took under her flag 245,000 square miles, the greater part of which, 190,000 square miles,

Veterans of Adowa: Left, Menelik II; right, the Warrior Empress, Taitu.
Center: The Ras Makonnen, father of Haile Selassie.

was ceded by England. For the remainder she paid $72,000 to the Sultan of Zanzibar.

Her next African grab was in her war with Turkey in 1911-12. From this Moslem power she took Tripoli—360,000 square miles—and Cyrenica—75,340. These were made into the Italian colony of Libya, with 580,000 square miles.

Italy in 30 years had acquired 870,534 square miles—a territory one-fourth the size of the United States and six times larger than herself.

But here's the rub: This vast empire was mostly rocky, arid, broiling desert, and worth less than a few acres of suburban New York. At best it was a liability. This was why Italy had been permitted by the other powers to have it. England, as was said, gave Italy most of the Somaliland territory, and when Britain cedes any territory you may be sure it is absolutely worthless and a burden.

But there was method in Italy's madness. Count Crispi, the Mussolini of 1894, saw again a great Italian empire stretching from Tunis across the way from Sicily to down the entire length of the Red Sea. Two of these worthless colonies, Erithrea and Somaliland touched Ethiopia, the first on the northeast, the second on the southeast. Standing on his hot, barren rocks, the Roman Wolf now cast greedy eyes upwards to where his rich, fertile neighbor, Ethiopia, lay in the cool, well-watered mountains. Europe had grabbed all of Africa save this prize. He licked his chops greedily. He would finish the job.

Let's go back to 1885. Italy, having squatted to the northeast of Ethiopia made it clear that she meant to annex the ancient empire simply by marching in and taking it as England, France, Belgium and Portugal had done other parts of Africa.

At the time Ethiopia was being torn with civil war. John, son of Theodore, a usurper, was at war with Menelik II, the rightful heir. Agostini Depretis, the Mussolini of that day, seized the opportunity to invade Ethiopia and annexed a choice portion, adjoining Erithrea. It was Menelik's land, but the robbery made John uneasy. After Menelik had been eaten his turn would be next.

Leaving his rival, John, Menelik marched against the Italians. Several skirmishes followed with Menelik, sometimes the victor, sometimes the Italians. On Jan. 14, 1887, Menelik captured Count Salembini, who had penetrated into the interior on a supposed scientific mission, and held him as a pledge that the Italians would quit his territory. They refused.

The Ethiopians, commanded by the Ras Alula, thereupon marched against the Italians, whose forces consisted of 512 whites and several thousand natives, under Col. Cristofori. They met at Dogali on Jan. 26, 1887. Surrounded by the Ethiopians, the Italians were thoroughly defeated, the only survivors being eighty-two wounded. On this the remaining Italians in Ethiopia retreated to the coast leaving behind their supplies. The moment seemed favorable for the Ethiopians to push Italy from East Africa, but they contented themselves with occupying the strategic posts. For the release of Salembini, Menelik demanded and obtained the release of a large supply of ammunition that Italy had captured at sea.

The defeat at Dogali by a black nation aroused deep anger and humiliation in Italy. Depretis was driven from office. Italy, burning for revenge, voted $6,000,000 for the war and sent out 12,000 well-equipped white troops, a large army in those days. Supplemented with 13,000 black troops, the Italian commander, General San Marzano entered Ethiopia in December, 1887, determined to conquer it once for all. In February, 1888, he cap*·ᵗred Saati and built a railroad linking it with Massowah. But when a clash s·emed near, the Ethiopian army suddenly retreated.

The reason was that their old foes, the Dervishes, or Mohammedans had invaded Ethiopia. The Italians, perhaps not knowing this and think ing it a trap, retreated to their territory also. But they returned in May 1888, and were defeated at Saganeiti. Again they quitted Ethiopian ter ritory.

These three failures made Italy realize why England and the other European powers hadn't gobbled Ethiopia. Britain, it is true, had invaded Ethiopia in 1867 as far as the mountain fortress of Magdala to punish the mad king, Theodore, for his seizure of English missionaries. This had been done, however, with the general consent of the Ethiopians and Britain had retired immediately taking with her some priceless Ethiopic manuscripts, and the Kebra Nagast, or Ethiopian Book of Kings, which had first been written in 400 B. C.

The Italians now attempted to gain their ends by craft and diplomacy. John and Menelik, being still at war, they decided to play one against the other after the manner in which Cortez with a handful of men had seized Mexico. General Barateri, the Italian commander visited Menelik and offered him arms to regain the throne of his ancestors. Similar overtures were made to John. Both accepted but with little intention of keeping their promises. Italy complains bitterly of the lack of Ethiopian faith. The simple truth is that there has been no faith involved on either side. It was a case of ruse against ruse with the Africans being the trickier of the two.

John and Menelik thought themselves justified when they saw the Italians nibbling at their territory. Finally when Barateri permitted the pillaging of Adowa by native troops, Menelik realized that no confidence whatever could be placed in him. What the Italians did not know, moreover, was that their aggression had driven John and Menelik together and that the two had made a treaty, whereby Menelik should be John's heir. To bind the bargain, John's son, the Ras Area, married Menelik's daughter, Zaiditu, or Judidth.

Soon after John was killed in battle with the Mahdi, a Negro prophet, who had driven England from the Soudan. Ras Mangascha, John's son claimed the Ethiopian throne, and civil war broke out again.

Count Crispi, then Premier, saw his opportunity. Crispi's dream, like that of Mussolini's, was an African empire stretching from Sicily to the Straits of Babel-Mandeb and taking in Tunis, Egypt, the Soudan, and Ethiopia. Accordingly he took advantage of the disorder to march into Ethiopia. At the same time he sent a mission, headed by Count Antonelli, to hail Menelik as the rightful sovereign, and to make a treaty with him.

This treaty, known as Outchale in Ethiopian and Ucciali in Italian, was signed in 1889. By its terms Italy lent Ethiopia 4,000,000 gold francs ($800,000), a half of which was to be in arms and ammunition. As security Italy was given control of the customs at Harrar, a rich coffee province. In case of non-payment. Harrar was to be ceded to Italy. Menelik, pressed by Mangascha, accepted these severe terms. Two copies of the Treaty of Outchale, Ethiopia had pledged to make all negotiations

Italy, now triumphantly announced to the European powers that Ethiopia was her protectorate. King Humbert of Italy sent 38,000 rifles and 28 modern cannon to his new "son" Menelik, who replied with a slice of land, known as Asmara.

The next four years were peaceful, despite continued Italian aggression on Ethiopian territory. Italy justified herself by deciding that she was dealing with an "inferior" people.

About 1892, Menelik was seized with the ambition to modernize his country as the Japanese were doing. He instituted a postal service and struck coins and stamps with his own effigy. To this Italy strongly objected.

Then he started to make treaties with Germany, Russia and Turkey, on which Italy exploded in wrath. She said that according to the terms of the Treaty of Outchale, Ethiopia had pledged to make all negotiations with the other powers through her.

Menelik objected vigorously. He pointed to Art. 17 of the treaty with the Amharic word, "itchalloutchal," which means, "may, if he pleases," use Italian diplomacy. The Italians insisted that in their copy the word was "must", use Italian diplomacy. Menelik submitted the treaty to the leading Oriental scholars of Europe and Africa. They agreed that he was right and that he had not made his country a protectorate of Italy.

Apropos of this: On December 18, 1895, the Marquis du Rudini, ex-Premier, admitted in the Italian Parliament that Menelik was right (See; Revue Francaise et Exploration, vol. XXI, p. 30, 1896).

Menelik, eager to maintain his long friendship with King Humbert of Italy, wrote him.

"I realize that the Amharic text and the Italian version of this article 17 differ. But in signing it I stipulated that Ethiopian affairs could be treated by Italian diplomacy on my invitation. I have never promised to have it done by Italy alone.

"Your Majesty ought to understand that no independent power could ever make such a concession. If you have the honor of your ally, Ethiopia, at heart, you'll change this.'

Italy, realizing what it would mean to her prestige in Europe, if she yielded to this black, and as she deemed it, barbarian people, replied through her envoy.

"King Humbert cannot yield. It would hurt the pride and dignity of his people."

Menelik, with the thought of his country's seven thousand years of independence, flashed back, "If you have your dignity, so have we."

The Empress Taitu, warrior wife of Menelik, added, "You wish to make us your pupils but that will never be."

"Your Majesty," said the Italian envoy, "this means war."

"Then let it come," replied Menelik firmly. "We cannot permit our integrity as the oldest Christian nation to be questioned, nor the right to govern ourselves in absolute independence."

Menelik's first step was to return the amount of the loan with three times the stipulated interest. He took care, however, to keep the arms and ammunition that his estranged "brother," Humbert had given him.

Crispi at once made extensive preparations for the conquest of Ethiopia. His Parliament voted $8,000,000 for the war. At the same time he sent heavy shipments of arms to Mangascha and all the chiefs hostile to Menelik.

Italy, already beaten back three times, was cautious about attacking Menelik, however, and sent an envoy to him, asking him to yield. Menelik, like Haile Selassie, pledged to fight to the last man rather than surrender.

In this crisis Menelik now showed that statemanship, which has placed him among the foremost leaders of modern times. He had conquered the greater part of Ethiopia and had reduced the chiefs to his will. Many of them were still angry with him. But assembling his messengers he sent

Veterans of Adowa. Above, left to right, the Ras Michael, father of the ex-Emperor Lidj Yassu; Ras Mangascha, son of King John. Below: Hapti Giorgis, Minister of War; and the Ras Alula, Chief Commander at Adowa.

them over the land to all the kings and chiefs urging them to unite against a foe who was going to take from them even such measure of independence as they had enjoyed under him. Did they want to submit to the white man who had seized and enslaved all the rest of Africa? They assembled at Boromeda. Menelik addressed them in stirring language. "Whatever be our differences we can never permit our country which has maintained its freedom for seventy centuries to be ruled by an outsider. You have seen what the white man has done to the rest of Africa. Do you, a proud fighting race, want to be enslaved like the other inhabitants of this continent? Ethiopia has never been conquered. And she shall never be as long as she preserves her indomitable spirit. Ethiopia shall stretch her hand only to God—and to smite her enemies."

All pledged their allegiance. The Ras Mangascha, Menelik's chief foe asked to be permitted to lead the attack. "I will drive out the Italians," he said, "with the very bullets they gave me to kill you."

Count Crispi now decided once for all on the conquest and annexation of Ethiopia, while England, France, Russia and Austria protested. Italy voted an additional $4,000,000 to carry on the war and sent out 15,000 more men.

To show his defiance, Crispi seized three Ethiopian princes who were studying engineering in Switzerland and held them as hostages over the protest of the Swiss.

Italy won at first. At Coatit and Senafe in 1895 she defeated Mangascha. Another victory at Delsa was telegraphed to Rome and magnified into a triumph. The war was already won!

But these successes were only a trap. Mangascha had been instructed to draw the enemy into the country away from his base, toward Menelik who was awaiting with 90,000 men.

On December 7, 1895, at Amba Alagi the advancing Italians, 5,200 strong, encountered the vanguard of the Ethiopian army which was commanded by the Ras Makonnen, and were killed to a man. Laying siege to the Italian stronghold at Makalle, Makonnen captured it, forced the Italians to pay $500,000, and to surrender all their arms.

The $500,000 had been paid for the ransom of the captured Italians. In returning these Menelik showed a strategy, which some military experts declare is without a parallel for shrewdness. He had the Ras Makonnen escort the prisoners to the Italian lines, at the same time giving the impression that he, himself, was going to attack Addigrat, another Italian post. But when half-way he changed his direction and marched on the main body of the Italian army. The first of these movements had served as a screen for the second and had completely fooled the Italian scouts.

Before Barateri was aware of it he found himself blocked by the main body of the Ethiopian army. Retreat was his only salvation. But since he could not be sure even of that he tried to make terms with Menelik. The latter demanded the payment of $12,000,000 and the evacuation of all Ethiopian territory.

For the next five weeks negotiations went on, while the two armies rested within eighteen miles of each other. The Italians had 20,521 men of whom 7,330 were natives, and 64 cannon. Menelik outnumbered them four to one. But his men had mostly spears. His 42 cannon were nearly all old style. The Ethiopians, great cavalry fighters—they were the first to use horses in warfare—had only 8,600 horses. A plague had killed nearly all their animals.

Faced with these conditions, Barateri telegraphed to Crispi making known his precarious position, and saying that should the enemy attack he hoped to be able to repulse him. But Crispi, who was faced by a similar crisis' at home, and wished to re-instate himself by a coup, sent a stinging reply.. He accused Barateri of suffering from "military rheumatism."

"Give me a decisive victory, or out you go," was his ultimatum.

On the night of February 29, 1896, Barateri took advantage of the moonlight and the fact that the next day was a great feast of the Ethiopians—that of St. George's—to advance.

Warned by his scouts, Menelik moved forward although a third of his men were away for the holiday. By using mountain passes unknown to the Italians he crept upon them and surrounded them almost entirely. At 6:30 the next morning the Italians opened the battle. Their mountain guns played havoc with the massed Ethiopians. But Menelik, bring-up his modern quick-firers replied with vigor. Then he gave the order to advance on all fronts, and the Ethiopians sweeping down, pressed the Italians into such a closely packed mass that they could not use their guns. Many of their cannon were found after the fight, unfired. Thereafter the battle was a massacre. The Ethiopians speared the foe like sheep. By 3:00 P. M. the Italians were in full flight, leaving 12,000 dead.

The Ethiopians did not pursue them but the black subjects of Italy, taking advantage of the defeat, slaughtered the fugitives.

Among the slain were two Italian generals, Dabormida and Arimondi. Albertone, a third, was captured with 7,000 men. The entire supplies, including the 56 cannon and 4,000,000 cartridges fell to Menelik, whose loss was between 3,000 and 5,000 slain.

The victory resounded around the world. It amazed Europe and heartened black men everywhere. Especially it gave to the oppressed Africans new hope.

There was a rush of the European powers to make treaties with Menelik. From being considered an insignficant barbarian, he became a figure of importance.

The Ras Alula, a really great commander, came in for high praise. Guglielmo Ferrero, an Italian, and one of Europe's leading historians, believes that Count Schiefflin, head of the German General Staff and author of the plan for the German offensive on Paris in 1914, endeavored to imitate Ras Alula's strategy at Adowa. Schiefflin credited it to Hannibal, says Ferrero, because Ras Alula was black and he did not wish to give credit to a black man (Hannibal, of course was also a Negro).

"The battle of Adowa," says Ferrero . . . "is a little known but brilliant case of surrounding on both wings . . . If we took Count Schiefflin's doctrines literally the greatest warrior in history would appear to be the Ras Alula, the general in command of the Abyssinian forces at Adowa. Ras Alula succeded where Napoleon and Hannibal had failed. With a Vernichtungslaat (a single drive) lasting one day the Ras Alula solved a vital problem for his country.

"Thanks to the battle of Adowa, the Ethiopian empire has lived for forty years unmolested by the imperialistic ambitions of the West" (N. Y. American, November, 1933).

In Italy the effect was terrific. Crispi was mobbed in Parliament by angry Italian mothers, and driven from office. Italian soldiers mutinied rather than go to Africa. When General Balciderra, the new Italian commander, declared that it would take an army of 250,000 men, $1,100,000,000, and five years to conquer Ethiopia, Italy was forced to recognize the absolute independence of Ethiopia and to pay an indemnity of 10,000,000 gold lira, which was then worth about $5,000,000.

Is it any wonder after these futile and costly attempts that Italy now shows such desperation in her efforts to grab Ethiopia. Of all the European nations she has had by far the worst luck in Africa. After this toll of lives and expenditure of money then and since her territory there is still almost worthless rock and burning sand.

On December 5, 1934, Italy resumed active aggression again. Walwal, where the present dispute began, is sixty miles within the Ethiopian border, even on the Italian maps. Italy now claims this as her ^territory asserting that Ethiopia has no well-defined borders. But a nation without them could not be admitted to the League. Count Bonin Longare, the Italian delegate, who sponsored Ethiopia's admission in 1923, when asked whether Ethiopia's borders were clearly marked, replied in the affirmative.

For full details of Ethiopia's admission into the League and the cordial attitude of Italy, then, as well as the discussion on slavery, see: League of Nations Official Journal, Special Supplement, No. 19, Geneva, 1923.

SLAVERY IN ETHIOPIA

SLAVERY in one form or another exists in nearly all Africa today. It was only in 1928 that the slaves of Sierra Leone, Britain's oldest African colony, were finally freed, or were said to be.

In Ethiopia slavery goes back to the most ancient times. It was also sanctioned by Mosaic law which Ethiopia still uses.

The first slaves in Ethiopia, as elsewhere, were prisoners of war, who were unable to pay ransom. These slaves begat slave children. Ethiopia, nearly always at war, continued to accumulate slaves.

Since the Ethiopian is a warrior by profession he shuns other work, hence slaves were needed to till the soil. There has also been a demand for slaves in Arabia from time immemorial. It is held that but for this importation of human beings the Arabian population would become extinct. Today the majority of slaves imported into Arabia come from Ethiopia and the Sudan.

Ethiopian, and other Oriental slavery, differ widely from American slavery. It is domestic servitude. The slaves, far more often than not, became a member of the family. Slaves who have children by the master, are not only freed, but the children are treated in all respects like the legal ones. A son by a slave mother might in time become the head of the family. Many rulers of the Mohammedan empire even at the height of its power had slave mothers. Indeed these were preferred in order to avoid political meddling by her family. Sometimes these slave mothers were Ethiopian.

Menelik, the greatest of the Ethiopian emperors, prior to Haile Selassie, had a slave mother, named Edgig Ayeihu. Ethiopian slavery was never as degrading as American slavery.

Beginning with Theodore, succeeding Ethiopian emperors have tried to abolish slavery in vain. It was too ingrained. Moreover African conditions forced many individuals to seek masters in order to get food and protection. Others voluntarily went to Mecca as pilgrims in order to sell themselves.

When Haile Selassie became regent he took steps to wipe out slavery.

Above: Left to right, Hapti Michael, Chief Commander of the Ethiopian Army (Photo by the author); and an Ethiopian grand dame. Below: Young Ethiopia.

It was, moreover, one of the conditions by which Ethiopia was admitted to the League. It was impossible, however, to bring about immediate emancipation because large numbers of the slaves had no homes. Turned adrift they would become either beggars or bandits. Many also refused to leave their masters.

Italy, herself, praised Haile Selassie for his fight against slavery when he had done far less than now. Count Bonin-Longare, Mussolini's delegate to the League of Nations, said: "One must, however, pay tribute, particularly to Ras Tafari (now Haile Selassie) present heir to the throne, a prince of broad views who is open to modern ideas and in whose praise one can mention the decree of November, 1918, reinforcing all previous edicts and punishing slave traffic severely.

"As regards the condition of the slaves, a gradual humanizing of habits of life has brought about an improvement in their position so that it is more appropriate to speak of serfs rather than of slaves."

The greatest evil of slavery is slave-raiding. Haile Selassie has fought this vigorously. He executes all slave-raiders caught. But Ethiopia has been no more successful against the boot-legging of slaves than the United States with all its power and wealth was against the liquor traffic.

Many Europeans are in collusion with the slave-traders. The greatest of the modern slave-dealers was a Frenchman. To reach Arabia, where slaves fetch a high price, one must pass through Italian, French or British territory. Ethiopia has no sea-coast. It means, therefore, that one or more of the European powers surrounding Ethiopia are lax about smuggling.

In 1935, Haile Selassie decreed a general emancipation, but slavery whether voluntary or forced will continue until there is an industrial change in Ethiopia.

Slavery cannnot be condoned even when it takes the disguised form of Fascism. But if we are inclined to be impatient with slavery in Ethiopia let us remember that although it was abolished in America seventy years ago that it survives as peonage in the United States today. Certain American States sell their prisoners to business concerns and pocket the money. And in order to get this revenue minor social misdemeanors of Negroes are magnified into offenses drawing heavy fine and imprisonment. Peonage in America is not only more harsh than slavery in Arabia and Ethiopia, but there is far less economic justification for it.

Finally a liberated Ethiopian slave becomes a man at once and loses the stigma of servitude. He may rise to a position inferior only to that of the emperor, as in the case of Hapti Giorgis, one of the greatest of the Ethiopian generals and a national hero. But in the United States the curse and the stigma of slavery is still visited on the great-great-grand-children of the ex-slaves.

———

For Haile Selassie's pronouncement on slavery and the decrees of the Ethiopian government respecting it see: League of Nations, series 6-B. No. 9, Geneva, May 14, 1924.

Kessell, J. Marches d'Esclaves. Paris.
Rutter, E. Holy Cities of Arabia. London, 1928.
Makin, W. J. Red Sea Nights. London, 1932.
Simon, Lady K. Slavery. London, 1929.
Slavery. League of Nations Publ. VI. B.1 1935.

For additional information on slavery and authorities see: Rogers -J. A. 100 Amazing Facts About the Negro and "The Key" (Slavery).

GEOGRAPHY, ECONOMIC CONDITIONS, ETC.

ETHIOPIA has an area of from 350,000 to 450,000 square miles, or larger than Italy, France and the State of New York combined. The population is estimated at from ten to twelve millions.

It is bordered, for the greater part, by desert, where the temperature reaches, in places, 150 degrees in the shade. In the uplands the climate ranges from a mild tropical to a semi-tropical, while some of the mountains are 15,000 feet and are snow-clad. Addis-Ababa, the capital, is 8,000 feet high. In the winter months the climate is heavenly with its bright sunshine and almost frosty nights.

Ethiopia is the most mountainous region in Africa with gorges perhaps deeper and vaster than any in the world. One of these, the Takasse, is larger than the Grand Canyon. Ethiopia's mountains have been her strength. She has been rightly called "The Switzerland of Africa."

There are many rivers, the largest of which is the Abai, or Blue Nile. Of the several large lakes, Tsana (not Tana) comes first with an area of 1,150 square miles. Two of these, Hora Abyata and Shala, are salt.

Ethiopia's natural resources are of the richest. First, at least in historical importance, is gold. It was the source of this metal for ancient Egypt. Its natives still wash gold in the same streams five thousand years later.

Western Ethiopia is rich in oil and so are parts of the eastern. There are also platinum, silver, iron, copper, coal, salt, tin, potash and other minerals.

Agriculture and cattle-rearing are the chief industries. The principal livestock are cows, horses, sheep, camels, mules and donkeys. The soil is exceedingly fertile producing corn, wheat, dhourra, barley, rye, peas, cotton, sugar-cane and all kinds of tropical fruit with little cultivation. Coffee grows wild in the provinces of Harrar and Caffa. Ethiopia is the original home of coffee.

Wild animals are abundant. The lion, symbol of Ethiopia, attains its largest size there. There are deer, zebras, wild oxen, elephants, hippopotamuses, rhinoceroses, leopards, hyenas and monkeys of various kinds in myriads. The Ethiopian giraffe is the tallest and finest in the world, and much sought after by zoological gardens. Menelik once used this fact to show his displeasure to nations having an alliance with Italy by forbidding exportations of Ethiopian giraffes to them.

Most varieties of tropical birds are also to be found there, including the ostrich.

There are several curative hot springs, one of the finest being at Addis-Ababa.

The principal exports are coffee, hides, skins and wax. The chief imports are cotton goods. Currency is the heavy Maria Theresa silver thaler, or dollar, which is worth about thirty American cents, though it is almost twice as large as the American dollar. In distant parts of the interior salt is used for small currency.

Ethiopian trade is at present insignificant. Its total imports and exports do not exceed $15,000,000 annually. When properly developed Ethiopia, with her fine climate and enormous natural resources, bids fair to become an earthly paradise.

THE ETHIOPIAN MAN

HE Ethiopians are brave, hardy, of fine physique and inured to war by thousands of years of self-defense. They are very mobile, being perhaps the swifest and most enduring runners on earth. They travel light, their commisseary being almost non-existent. Cattle are driven along with the army, and killed and eaten raw to avoid the enemy's seeing their smoke. Parched grain is carried in a knapsack. Their tents and blankets are mother-earth.

In strategy the African has been renowned since the days of Hannibal of Carthage. In the clash at Walwal, December 5, 1934, the Ethiopian commander drove his cattle against the Italian tanks putting them to confusion as Hannibal did the Romans, or Cetewayo, Zulu king, did the British in 1879.

THE ETHIOPIAN WOMAN

HE Ethiopian woman enjoys a greater degree of independence than those of any other land. She is complete mistress of her body and her property.

She has four kinds of marriage from which to choose. One is a contract for two years, another is a civil union of indeterminate length. If the first is successful it usually leads to the second.

But if it is not she may free herself from either at any time, without expense, merely by calling in a disinterested person to act as judge.

The third is a church marriage. This is usually taken only by couples who through the years have grown to feel that they were made for each other. From this there is no divorce.

In the fourth a woman hires herself as a combination wife and servant by the year. But all these different marriages must be sworn to before a priest and regular witnesses. Naturally as Ethiopia is composed of several peoples, who differ in customs and in religion, there are exceptions to the above.

An Ethiopian woman may bring her husband to court even for calling her a bad name, have him fined, and pocket the fine. And she needs no witnesses as Ethiopian women have the reputation of being the most truthful in the world.

She goes with her husband to war, and often becomes his avenger, should he fall. Usually she is fiercer in battle than the man. Europeans sometimes kill themselves, rather than fall into the hands of the African woman.

Queen Taitu, wife of Menelik, was a famous warrior. She led her own troops to battle against the Italian at Adowa, and spurred on the men by her valiant conduct.

THE SEX LURE OF ETHIOPIA

N addition to the economic there is another lure of the Italians in Ethiopia which cannot be ignored. That is the sex lure—the prospects of having Ethiopian girls. Already novels are appearing in Italy whose heroes are sturdy young Fascisti and whose heroines are beautiful Ethiopians. According to the Associated Press the Fascists in East Africa want to marry the dusky maidens but Mussolini objects.

There are hundred of mulattoes now in Ethiopia by Italian fathers. One of the great attractions that Africa holds for the white man has been the abundance of black women in a nude or semi-nude state, as Mary

Gaunt and other African travellers have said.

The lure of the black woman also played an important part in the American Civil War. David Goodman Croly, a white editor of that time, declared that one of the principal reasons why the Southern men fought to preserve slavery was that they feared that freedom would deprive them of sexual domination over the Negro women.

BRITAIN'S BOND TO ETHIOPIA

THIOPIA is of the first strategic importance to the British Empire. To her east is the Red Sea, which is the life-line of Britain; to her west is the Cape-to-Cairo Railway, aptly described as Britain's spinal cord in Africa; in Ethiopia's centre is Lake Tsana, the source of the Blue Nile as well as the sources of other rivers, which if diverted would make British territory to the north and all Egypt almost a Sahara, or at least as worthless as the Italian possessions in Africa.

In control of Ethiopia, Italy would be a menace to the other white powers already there. By training and arming the warlike Ethiopians she could conquer the surrounding territory; cut off England from India, Australia, and her colonies in the Far East; imperil France on both shores of the Mediterranean; and be dominant in Europe. Mussolini is a far greater menace to world peace than the Kaiser.

Having failed to seize Ethiopia, Britain is now firm for her independence and in all her treaties with England and France regarding Ethiopia has always insisted on this.

WHAT THE ETHIOPIANS MIGHT EXPECT UNDER ITALIAN RULE

HOULD the Italians ever dominate Ethiopia, the Ethiopians may expect the same treatment that the Italians meted out to the natives of Tripoli since 1911. The Tripolitan tribesmen who were as determined to guard their independence as the Ethiopians are, were butchered in a manner unparalleled in modern times. On October 29, 1911, during the Turco-Italian war, 4,000 non-combatants, including women and children were massacred. For a recital of this horror not from one news correspondent, but several, see F. McCullagh's "Italy's War for a Desert", Part IV. "The Massacres", pp. 246-395. Also the N. Y. Times, October 31 and November 1, 1911.

In January, 1932, another appalling butchery occurred. Having built 180 miles of barb wire to hem in the Senussi, the Italians herded, it is said, some fifty thousand of them together, and then showered bombs on them from the air, utterly wiping them out. This atrocity caused the greatest indignation throughout Islam. (N. Y. Times, May 3; December 16, 1931 and January 27, 1932.)

Ruthless at home, Fascism has introduced some new horrors in her colonizing in Africa.

HAILE SELASSIE I
(Power of the Holy Trinity)

AILE SELASSIE I, King of Kings of Ethiopia, last of the independent sovereigns of Africa, and now centre of the world's attention, was born on July 17, 1891, according to the Western calendar, or 1883, according to the Ethiopian one. His father was the Ras Makonnen, a nephew of Menelik, who distinguished himself in the victorious war against Italy in 1896.

Haile Selassie was an extraordinarily bright youth and showed great promise of statesmanship at an early age. At fourteen he was the Governor of Garamoulta, which post he relinquished on the death of his father to reside at the court of Menelik.

There he continued his studies under Ethiopian and European tutors. Then Menelik appointed him governor of Basso which post he filled with such competence that he was made administrator of Harrar, the most important province of Ethiopia, while he was not yet twenty.

At this time he nearly lost his life. While crossing Lake Arumuya with seven others the boat capsized. He swam ashore; the rest were drowned.

As the result of political intrigue he was removed from Harrar and sent to the distant province of Caffa, but thanks to his skill and his integrity he was soon restored to Menelik's favor.

On Menelik's death, Lidj Yassu, Menelik's grandson, came to the throne. Lidj Yassu's father, the Ras Michael, was a Mohammedan, and Lidj Yassu too, showed Islamic sympathies. He took several wives, wore the fez, and sided with the "Mad" Mullah, a Mohammedan prophet, who had driven the British from all of Somaliland save the coast.

Ethiopia's policy for 1,600 years has been a Christian one. As the King of England pledges himself to maintain Protestantism so the Emperor of Ethiopia must swear to uphold Christianity. Lidj Yassu by his observance of Mohammedan customs was thus violating Ethiopian law.

During the war of 1914, Lidj Yassu also sided with Germany and tried to bring about a union of Christian and Mohammedan against England and her allies. Since Ethiopia is of strategic importance to Britain the maintenance of Christianity in Ethiopia and her friendliness to England are of vital political importance to the welfare of the British empire. Hostility to Britain might have meant war against Ethiopia. Therefore the Abuna, or head of the Ethiopian church, and the Ethiopian leaders deposed Lidj Yassu. In his place they put Zauditu, or Judith, a daughter of Menelik, Haile Selassie (then the Ras Tafari) was named heir to the throne and regent.

Lidj Yassu's father, the Ras Michael, gathered a large army and marched against the Christians. In a great battle fought at Sagalle on October 27, 1916, the Ras Michael was totally defeated. Haile Selassie, who was one of the Christian commanders, distinguished himself by his generalship and his valor.

When Lidj Yassu gathered another army in 1921, Haile Selassie marched against him, captured him, and held him prisoner, which he still is.

In 1923, Haile Selassie again showed his statesmanship by maneouvering himself into the League of Nations, despite the opposition of England, Australia, Holland, Norway and Lithuania, but with the support of France, Italy, Portugal, Belgium and the Latin-American nations. Hereafter none of the European powers would be able to absorb Ethiopia without breaking

Above: Belaten Gheta Herouy, Foreign Minister; H. R. H., the Duke of Glou-ster; the interpreter, son of the Foreign Minister; H. M. Haile Selassie; and Gen. ergine, at Addis-Ababa. (Photo by the author.)

Below: Haile Selassie; Lidj Yassu, deposed Emperor; and Ras Birru, who is w on a mission to Japan.

the Covenant of the League. The great wisdom of this move is now being demonstrated.

In 1924 he toured Europe with an imposing retinue of thirty Rases, or princes, with their trains. Some of these were his secret enemies, who were plotting to take his place, and he took them along so that he could keep his eyes on them.

In England he was received by King George at Buckingham Palace and dined there. Cambridge University conferred on him the degree of LL.D. King Albert of Belgium, Victor Emmanuel of Italy, the President of France, and other rulers received him with the honors due the heir to a throne.

On his return to Ethiopia he tried to modernise the ancient empire. He introduced the telephone, and the airship; built a wireless station and sent promising Ethiopian youths to be trained in France, Germany, England. and the United States, looking forward to the day when the great natural resources of Ethiopia would be developed by her own mechanics, engineers, scientists, and aviators. In these efforts he worked from sixteen to eighteen hours a day—a great feat in a hot climate. He knew that in order to win. the sympathy and good will of the world he must head off the charge that he was permitting rich territory fit for "white" habitation to remain in a backward state.

In addition he took steps to modernise the form of government from the old patriarchal one, and remodelled the police and the army.

All of this was done under great opposition from the Empress and her party. The latter held that the old customs were good enough, hoping by the preservation of them to curb European influence which has proved so disastrous to the freedom of the African peoples. Haile Selassie, on the other hand, thought it was possible to adopt beneficial European customs and inventions, and at the same time keep European influence within bounds. Perhaps he would prefer even less of this as he has said, "We need European progress only because we are surrounded by it. That is at once a benefit and a misfortune."

In 1928, the leaders of Ethiopia in recognition of his services appointed him Negus, or King, and he was crowned in October of that year. Nominal power still remained in the hands of the Empress Zaiditu. That same year he concluded a treaty of perpetual peace with Italy.

In 1930, the Ras Guksa, the husband of the Empress revolted. Haile Selassie marched against him, and defeated him, the Ras Guksa being among the slain.

The news of her husband's death killed Zaiditu and Haile Selassie succeeded to the throne, and was crowned amid great ceremonies and festivity at Addis-Ababa on November 2, 1930. Among those present at the coronation were the Duke of Gloucester, son of George V; the Duke of the Udine, nephew of Victor Emmanuel of Italy; and the Marshal Franchet d'Esperey of France.

But the accession to full power gave Haile Selassie by no means a free hand to carry out his reforms. He had first of all to contend with the great Rases, or rulers of provinces, who were as jealous of their power as the various states of the American union are of theirs. Some of the chiefs were subject only in name, and were actually hostile, while the lack of roads and communications made it impossible for the emperor to check them at short notice. Wild tribesmen profited by these, too, to invade the territory of adjoining nations, thus bringing reproach on the central power, and causing the payments of indemnities.

Another internal obstacle was the swarming Ethiopian clergy, which is very powerful, and ultra-conservative, and eager to keep the people in ignorance to serve its own ends. The venality, and superstition of this clergy is amazing. Today, like the clergy of the Middle Ages it opposes all scientific innovation and progress and even modern methods of healing.

Haile Selassie also had to contend with incessant foreign intrigue for the economic control, and even the direct seizure, of his country that went on not only abroad but in Ethiopia itself.

His economic difficulties were tremendous. Ethiopia, though rich in natural resources, is yet in the stage of primitive agriculture. Her coinage, such as Haile Selassie found it, was unstable and being of silver was of small value in the purchase of modernising implements in the gold countries. Further, such reforms are usually effected by foreign loans, but Ethiopian policy is not to borrow abroad. Haile Selassie knows that the first step towards losing his independence would be to owe money to Europe or America. Money to carry out his reforms has been and still is his great handicap.

Yet working under these and other disadvantages, he has instituted a Parliament and modern courts, has built roads, hospitals, schools, installed electric lighting in the streets, improved the commerce and international relations, all the while steering a diplomatic course between opposing factions and religions in his own land.

As for his daily duties they are manifold. He receives the diplomats of the various nations, attends to some minute details of the government or the army; gives orders and inspects the erection of a building or the installation of machinery, and the like, all in addition to being the chief justice of the empire. Each subject, however lowly, has the right of direct appeal to the Emperor. In the meantime he keeps an almost housewifely eye for other details. Passing along in his red Rolls Royce he will sometimes descend to instruct the Gouragi road-workers and might lift a stone, himself, to put it in the proper place. Truly he is the guiding spirit of his nation in the fullest sense of the word. He is the rare spectacle nowadays of the monarch being the greatest in the land not only in name but in worth, ability, and vision. Even more than Mussolini, he is the maker of his country.

As one writer has said, "The weight of the whole empire rests upon the shoulders of this quiet but iron-hearted little sovereign.

"Night and day he is beset by a thousand different problems and a thousand different worries and perplexities. Even while he eats he transacts state business. Even while he sleeps he has no respite.

"His secretary sleeps at the foot of his majesty's bed, ready at any moment to take the Emperor's orders in the event his majesty awakens and thinks about something he had forgotten during the day.

"Under terrific strain, he is trying almost overnight to transform his medieval empire into a modern state."

Astonishment will increase when it is known that like Napoleon and Ghandi, he is a small man. Haile Selassie is barely over five feet tall, and weighs, it seems, not over a hundred and twenty pounds.

Haile Selassie's outstanding accomplishment, however, has been his fight against slavery, which had existed in Ethiopia from time immemorial. He began by freeing all the slaves in his palace; after which he made laws for the gradual emancipation of the remainder in the empire. He provided free education and clothing for the children of slaves and ex-slaves, together with appointment to government posts, depending upon individual ability; founded an anti-slavery society and an anti-slavery court; and made slave-raiding punishable with death. In 1935 he issued a proclamation wiping out slavery forever. In all his reforms Haile Selassie has had to go slow. He cannot change the psychology of his people or educate them overnight. One recalls the fate of King Amanuallah of Afghanistan, who tried to hasten progress in his own land. Moreover, most of Haile Selassie's people are anti-European in their ways. They know that the Europeans are ever scheming to take away their land as they did all the rest of Africa.

In disposition he is firm. His countrymen call him "Arko" (The Vise) for when he believes he is right he stands firm. In March, 1935, when Mussolini demanded a diplomatic apology, an indemnity, and the saluting of the Italian flag at Addis-Ababa over the Walwal incident, Haile Selassie sent him a flat refusal. And he did the unprecedented thing of giving out his reply to the press before he gave it to Italy thus giving Mussolini no chance to make it appear otherwise to the Italian people.

When George Bernard Shaw suggested that he yield to Italy and become a protectorate, he replied.

"I would rather kill myself, like Emperor Theodore sixty years ago, than become a puppet prince under the Italians

"I would be unworthy of my great ancestors, beginning with Solomon, if I submitted to Italian vassalage. Nor can I, as Sovereign of the oldest empire in the world, which had its beginnings before the Flood, accept a British protectorate or an Anglo-French regime.

"We cannot cut up Ethiopia like a cake, handing sugared parts to this and that country just to win their smiles and satisfy their sweet tooth.

"Would England or any other sovereign nation give up territory so willingly? No! I have taken an oath to the memory of the great Menelik to defend the empire until God calls me unto Him."

In manners, Haile Selassie is pleasing and most affable, yet full of dignity. His face radiates intelligence, serenity, kindliness, good nature and immense reserves of power. He smiles frequently, seeming at all times perfectly at ease. A Christian at heart, he observes the high principles of that faith. When a man who had tried to assassinate him was sentenced to death, Haile Selassie not only refused to sign the warrant, but forgave him. He has also abolished public hangings; mutilation for habitual thieves; and is endeavoring to supplant the old Mosaic law by which a murderer is handed over to the victim's next of kin, with modern law. But it is also said that he never forgets an enemy.

In features he is Oriental, a fact accentuated by his beard. In color he is a lightish black-brown, and considerably darker than one would infer from the published pictures of him. In reality he is what one would call in the United States a dark mulatto, judged both by his color and his hair. In his general expression he has been aptly described by one writer as a "black edition of the pictured Christ."

In his family life Haile Selassie differs from most Oriental monarchs; he has no concubines and only one wife. In 1912 he married Weyzero Menen, who has borne him five children. The Empress is a great granddaughter of Menelik, and a niece of the deposed emperor.

HOW DO THE ETHIOPIANS FEEL
TOWARDS THE AFRAMERICANS?

UT the Ethiopians do not consider themselves Negroes, many Aframericans will say. This is true. They object to the word, and so for that matter do many Aframericans, not to mention the Aframericans south of the Rio Grande, who do not use it.

A leading Ethiopian once said to this writer, "We think of ourselves as a nation, not as a race. This does not mean that we do not recognise our kinship with peoples of African descent in the New World. We wish you would urge as many as possible of your skilled farmers, mechanics, and scientists to come to Ethiopia. We need them here and would give them land free."

Ethiopia has always shown her friendliness to such Aframericans as have visited her. Menelik had a black West Indian, Dr. Vitalien, as his personal physician and adviser. He warmly welcomed Sylvain, the Haitian poet, and Daniel R. Alexander, a missionary, who still resides at Addis-Ababa.

Three different missions to the United States tried to get trained Aframericans in vain.

In 1930 Haile Selassie appointed Dr. J. B. West of Washington, D. C., as his personal physician. He gave Hubert Julian a large sum of money, made him a colonel in his army, and conferred on him the Gold Order of Menelik. He has made John Robinson of Chicago one of his principal aviators, and is using Aframerican world war veterans as drill-masters.

Lastly in one of his declarations Haile Selassie has announced that he is the head not only of Ethiopia, but of all peoples of African descent everywhere.

Aframericans in Ethiopia will be well-received provided that they do not go there with airs of superiority, and that they remember that the Ethiopians, never having been under white domination, look upon themselves exactly as white Americans or Englishmen do themselves in their own land.

Besides there will be a mutual economic benefit for both Aframericans and Ethiopians. The Ethiopians lack education and training and are hungering for it, preferably from teachers of their own color. The Aframerican needs an outlet for his trained youth. And if the economic depression lasts in America opportunities for skilled Negroes will become increasingly less. Ethiopia offers a vast outlet for Aframerican energies and Negro youths need have no longer any hesitancy in training themselves in engineering and other mechanical sciences.

Amharic, the official Ethiopian language, should be taught in Negro schools. Skilled Negroes should form a society in order to arrange for employment with the Ethiopian government.

HAILE SELASSIE AND MUSSOLINI CONTRASTED

NOTHING could be more striking than the difference between Haile Selassie and Mussolini

Mussolini glorifies war. His method of settling with a rival is to threaten him, and if that fails, kill him. Haile Selassie cultivates peace. His way of removing a rival is by conciliation. Born to autocratic power, Haile Selassie has voluntarily relinquished it, and is endeavoring to make Ethiopia a democracy. Mussolini, born under a constitutional monarchy, and once a Socialist, himself, has turned his country into an autocracy worse than under any sultan or czar. Haile Selassie belongs to the oldest family in the world, royal or otherwise. He is descended from King Ori of 4470 B. C. He can name all the rulers, his ancestors, who came after Ori. Despite this super-aristocrative lineage and the fact that he is invested with power more absolute than Mussolini was able to seize, he is modest, quiet, unassuming, affable and utterly without pose.

This writer has observed Haile Selassie for hours at a time—at military reviews, at the races, at public ceremonies, in his palace—and it has struck him that Haile Selassie in his every move was a gentleman-born, a true aristocrat.

Mussolini, on the other hand, is the direct descendant of a family that has been peasants for three centuries. His father was a blacksmith. He, himself, was a poor school-master, who through his ability rose to supreme power in his native land. While we know that character, not birth, is the principal force in the making of great men and that servants sometimes make able and considerate masters, Mussolini exhibits all the odious traits of the servant who has risen to authority, against which we are warned in the Bible. He is a strutter, poseur, braggart, and breather of defiance. His every move and gesture is calculated to impress the rabble. He is perpetually showing off. As Abdullah, King of Transjordania, recently said: "Mussolini's manner of speaking and the way he appears in photographs make me imagine him to be a cheap comedian."

This writer has also watched Mussolini in action at the Palazzio Venezia in Rome—shooting up his hand, pouting, grimacing, puffing out cheeks like a porcupine fish, gesturing, and otherwise clowning.

Great events would seem at times to prepare and train the men that are to handle them. For the American Revolution there was a Washington and for the Civil War a Lincoln. What might have happened to America but for these men? So it is with Ethiopia. The hand of destiny through difficult mazes brought Haile Selassie to supreme power. There were others, who were nearer to the throne than he. Now he stands forth as a wise and peerless leader. He is not only the foremost Ethiopian, but the leading individual of African descent. Indeed, it is not too much to say that he is the foremost living statesman.

In his address to Parliament on July 18, 1935, he said:

"We have always believed that a government ennobles, not debases itself when it voluntarily submits a quarrel to the judgment, perhaps the condemnation, of a qualified impartial international body."

Here is a model for all future statesmen to follow. With such an attitude wars will be no more. Thousands of years ago Ethiopia gave to the world the first ideal of right and wrong—the first morality. Today across the dim centuries Haile Selassie again points the way to interracial and international amity and brotherhood, which is the true goal of civilisation.

For a list of the Ethiopian kings from Ori of 4470 B. C. to Haile Selassie, see: Rey, C. F. In the Country of the Blue Nile, pp. 263-274, London, 1927.

Above: Her Majesty, the Empress Menen.   Below: The Emperor's retreat at Bishoftou.

WHAT ARE ETHIOPIA'S CHANCES
OF VICTORY

E refrain purposely from making any prediction as to Ethiopia's chances of success in a war with Italy. Ethiopia has an estimated total of 1,160,000 fighting men of whom only 237,000 have any degree of modern training. The latter are disposed as follows: the army of Ras Kassa of Beghie-Medir, 50,000; of Ras Emerou of Godjam, 50,000; of Ras Nessibu of Harrar, 20,000; of the Crown Prince, Asfa Wosen, 40,000; and the well-trained Imperial Guard of 7,000.

But Ethiopia has allies against which tanks, airplanes, and poison- gas will be useless. They are sun-stroke; burning, waterless deserts; towering peaks; gorges and ravines a mile deep; no roads; wide rivers to be bridged; sand storms; lack of sanitary drinking water; poisoned wells; tropical downpours that make the ground as slippery as soap; insects, whose bites cause irritation, disease, and death; malaria and other tropical maladies; and the pressure of the high altitudes.

If the Ethiopians adopt guerilla tactics the heavy armament of the Italians will lack the important objective for which such force was designed. It will be like using an elephant-gun to shoot a mosquito or a giant his full strength to throw a feather. As in the war against Abdel-Krim in Morocco, airplanes will serve chiefly in removing the wounded, while the heavy metal containers used for poison gas will prove largely to be- but so much impedimenta. The Italians took twenty-one years (1911-1932) to subdue the desert tribes of Cyrenaica, who were less than 230,000, were much nearer home, and on less difficult terrain.

In a long war Ethiopia's great peril may be lack of food. She has never had cause to lay in a supply. She has now an estimate of 21,000,000 head of cattle. But the Italians will undoubtedly use their airplanes to destroy the Ethiopian grain-fields and herds.

Ethiopia, Conquering Lion of the Tribe of Judah, saw the rise and the fall of the Pharaohs. She saw the empires of Cambyses, Darius, Cyrus and Alexander the Great melt into nothingness. She saw the glory that was Greece and the grandeur that was Rome become heaps of stone. This most ancient of the nations saw the rising and the setting of the Caesars of the West and of the East. She saw the birth of Islam, witnessed its sweep across the entire Old World, and aided in its check. She saw the rise and decline of. the Holy Roman Empire and the discovery of the New World. She saw black men become slaves in the New World and again win their freedom. She beheld the rise and the fall of Portugal, Spain, Holland, Sweden; was present at Napoleon's rise to power and his eclipse; as also that of the German Kaiser. She played the leading role in the downfall of two previous Mussolinis—Depretis and Crispi—and by the aid of her strong right arm and dauntless spirit she will also see the discomfiture and disgrace of this latest menace to world peace and brotherhood—Mussolini.

FOR GENERAL READING

Rey, C. F.—Unconquered Abyssinia, London, 1923.
Gruehl, M.—Citadel of Ethiopia, London, 1932.
Baum, J. E.—Savage Abyssinia, London, 1927.
Walker, C. H.—The Abyssinian at Home, London, 1933.
McCreagh, G.—The last of free Africa.
Gruehl, M.—Citadel of Ethiopia, London, 1932.
Nesbitt, L.—The Hell Hole of Creation, N. Y. 1932.

ETHIOPIA'S CHIEF NEED

IF civilization is a necessity of Ethiopia then Haile Selassie is by far the most logical leader of his own people, and Mussolini the least. In the present state of mind of the Ethiopians, the Italians will find no co-operation and must use coercion. Moreover, if the abolition of slavery is Italy's goal, she has failed in this respect in her North African colonies. In April, 1935, she was forced to admit at the League of Nations that slavery existed in Libya. Her report said, "In the zones controlled by us it was not possible, however, to extirpate the residual form of slavery that subsisted—essentially slavery of a domestic character. The old slaves continued to live in the families in which they already were, some of them refusing to leave their former masters . . .

"The present situation as regards domestic servitude is uniform throughout the colony . . .

"These remnants of domestic slavery will gradually disappear." (League of Nations Publications. Slavery. I. B.1, pp. 100-101).

In short this sounds like the same promises that Haile Selassie are making to get rid of slavery if given time.

It is true that the Amhara, or ruling class, has been oppressive—a condition that the Emperor is striving hard to correct. But if the Italians ever take control, the oppressed will have cause to long for the good old days of paternal slavery. As the New York Post says editorially:

"Fishing, farming and hunting are still free. So it is not economically necessary for the natives to work for a few pennies a day for some great Italian corporation. Italy, if it conquers Ethiopia, will remedy this. The farm land will be taken away from the peasants. Prohibitive taxes will be put on fishing and hunting. Slavery will no longer be necessary. Ethiopians will have to work or starve, and their masters will be relieved of the obligation to feed them when there is no work.

"Just as in civilized Italy."

Given the money, Haile Selassie and his people seem perfectly capable of working out their own salvation, and establishing the form of civilization best adapted to their country.

270421-300-11-60W

CPSIA information can be obtained
at www.ICGtesting.com
Printed in the USA
BVHW051253130223
658403BV00003B/416

PAGAN ORIGINS
of the
CHRIST MYTH

BY

JOHN G. JACKSON

ISBN: 9781639233199

Printed: December 2021

Cover Art By: Paul Amid

Published and Distributed By:
Lushena Books
607 Country Club Drive, Unit E
Bensenville, IL 60106
www.lushenabks.com

ISBN: 9781639233199

PAGAN ORIGINS
of the
CHRIST MYTH

BY

JOHN G. JACKSON

THE TRUTH SEEKER COMPANY, INC.
38 Park Row, New York, N. Y.

First printing, 1941: 4,000 *copies*
PRINTED IN THE UNITED STATES OF AMERICA

PAGAN ORIGINS OF THE CHRIST MYTH

THE cardinal doctrines of the Christian religion are, (1) the Fall of Man and (2) the Atonement. There are liberal Christian apologists who no longer subscribe to a literal belief in the Fall of Man. They have relegated Adam and Eve to the realm of mythology. These liberals are opposed by the orthodox apologists, who declare that belief in the Atonement implies belief in the Fall of Man. Logic seems to be on the orthodox side. As T. W. Doane has pointed out: "These two dogmas cannot be separated from each other. If there was no Fall, there is no need of an Atonement, and no Redeemer is required. Those then who consent in recognizing in Christ Jesus a God and Redeemer, and who, notwithstanding, cannot resolve upon admitting the story of the Fall of Man to be historical, should exculpate themselves from the reproach of inconsistency." ("Bible Myths," p. 17.)

Anyone who is familiar with the elements of the higher criticism knows that there are two stories of the Creation and Fall of Man in the Book of Genesis. The first, or Priestly Account, was written in the 5th century B.C., and extends from the beginning of Genesis through verse 3 of Chapter II. The second, or Jehovistic Account, begins with verse 4 of Chapter II, and extends through the 3rd chapter. This version of the story was written in the 8th century B.C. It is interesting to note that the second narrative is about 300 years older than the first. In the following comparison of these two tales, the Priestly version is designated by the letter P, and the Jehovistic version by the letters J. E. These documents differ in six important points, to wit:

(1) P: The earth emerges from the waters. It is saturated with moisture.

   J. E: The world at first a dry plain. There was no vegetation, because "the Lord God had not caused it to rain upon the earth." (Gen. II, 5.)

(2) P: Birds and beasts created before man.

   J. E: Man created before the birds and beasts.

(3) All fowls that fly are made out of the waters.

   J. E: The fowls of the air are made out of the ground.

(4) P: Man is created in the image of God.

   J. E: Man is made out of the dust of the ground. It is only after the eating of the forbidden fruit that the Lord God said:—"Behold, the man has become as one of us."

(5) P: Man made lord of the whole earth.

   J. E: Man merely placed in the garden to dress it and keep it.

(6) P: Man and Woman created together, as the closing and completing work of the whole creation.

   J. E: Man created first, then beasts and birds, which are named by the man. Finally, the woman is made out of a rib of the man.

Orthodox Christians claim that both of these stories must be believed, even though they contradict each other at numerous points. There have been eminent Christian authorities, however, who have rejected a literal view of Genesis. The celebrated church father, Bishop Origen, (185-253 A.D.), wrote as follows:

"What man of sense will agree with the statement that the first, second and third days, in which the evening is named and the morning, were without sun, moon and stars? What man is found such an idiot as to suppose that God planted trees in Paradise like a husbandman? I believe every man must hold these things for images under which a hidden sense is concealed."

St. Augustine, (354-430 A.D.), declared that: "There is no way of preserving the first chapter of Genesis without impiety, and attributing things to God unworthy of him." There is, of course, nothing unique about these Hebraic Eden myths. They were known among the so-called heathens thousands of years before the Bible was invented. Two very fine examples are cited by Sir Godfrey Higgins, the English orientalist, as follows:

(1). "A striking instance is recorded by the very intelligent traveller, Wilson, regarding a representation of the Fall of our first parents, sculptured in the magnificent temple of Ipsambul, in Nubia. He says that a very exact representation of Adam and Eve in the Garden of Eden is to be seen in that cave, and that the serpent climbing around the tree is especially delineated, and the whole subject of the tempting of our first parents most accurately exhibited." ("Anacalypsis," Vol. I, p. 403.)

(2). "A drawing brought by Colonel Coombs from a sculptured column in a cave temple in the south of India, represents the first pair at the foot of the ambrosial tree, and a serpent entwined among the heavily-laden boughs, presenting them some of the fruit from his mouth." ("Anacalypsis," Vol. I, p. 404.)

Mr. George Smith, of the Department of Oriental Antiquity of the British Museum, discovered Assyrian terra cotta tablets in the ruins of Nineveh, dating from 1500 to 2000 B.C., which give not only the story of the Creation of Man, but narratives of the Deluge and the Tower of Babel as well. In referring to an engraving on an Assyrian cylinder, Mr. Smith notes that: "One striking and important specimen of early type in the British Museum collection has two figures sitting one on each side of a tree, holding out their hands to the fruit, while at the back of one (the woman) is scratched a serpent . . . thus it is evident that a form of the Fall, similar to that of Genesis, was known in early times in Babylonia." ("The Chaldean Account of Genesis," p. 91, N. Y., 1876.)

In the original Babylonian Eden myth, as translated from a Sumerian tablet by Professor Edward

Chiera; there is the story of a great conflict among the gods. They cannot decide whether man ought to be created or not. A wise old reptile, the dragon Tiamat, opposed the creation of the human race. The Dragon fought against the great god Bel. Finally the god overcame the dragon by blasting him with thunderbolts. Opposition having been crushed, man was created. This conflict between Bel and the Dragon bears a close analogy to the story of the Revolution in Heaven recorded in the Apocalypse: "And there was war in heaven: Michael and his angels fought against the dragon; and the dragon fought and his angels, and prevailed not; neither was their place found anymore in heaven. And the great dragon was cast out, that old serpent, called the devil, and Satan, which deceiveth the whole world; he was cast out into the earth, and his angels were cast out with him." (Revelation, XII, 7-9.)

The myths of the Fall are based on man's yearning for immortality. Due to the habit of certain species of snakes of periodically shedding their skins, primitive man got the idea that serpents were immortal. The natural vanity of man told our distant ancestors that the gods had intended the gift of eternal life for humanity alone. So the serpent was conceived of as having stolen the precious prize from the human race. The Biblical version of the Fall of Man is incomplete. The role of the serpent is not explained, and the Tree of Life is not given due prominence in the story. The original story, which we are able to piece together from fragments gathered from the mythology of many lands, reads as follows: God placed the first man and woman in a garden of delights. In this garden were two trees, the Tree of Life and the Tree of Death (called the Tree of Knowledge in the Bible). Man had the choice of eating the fruit of the Tree of Life and becoming immortal, or of eating the fruit of the Tree of Death and becoming mortal. God sent the serpent to tell Adam and Eve to eat of the fruit of the Tree of Life, so that they might live forever, and to warn them against eating of the fruit of the Tree of Death, for if they should eat this forbidden fruit they would surely die, and this curse would descend to their children from generation to generation. The wily serpent, however, reversed the message. He told the first human pair that they would obtain immortality by eating of the fruit of the Tree of Death. Unfortunately Adam and Eve believed the diabolical snake, ate the forbidden fruit, and as a consequence were expelled from Eden and became mortal. The sly reptile, on the other hand, helped himself to the fruit of the Tree of Life and gained immortal life for himself and his kind. For a masterly study of myths concerning the fall of man, the reader is referred to Sir James George Frazer's "Folklore in the Old Testament," Vol. I. Frazer holds that the Hebrews got their version, directly or indirectly from Africa: "Even if the story should hereafter be found in a Sumerian version this would not absolutely exclude the hypothesis of its African origin, since the original home of the Sumerians is unknown. . . . In favor of an African origin of the myth it may be observed that the explanation of the supposed immortality of serpents, which probably furnished the kernel of the story in its original form, has been preserved in several African versions, while it has been wholly lost in the Hebrew version; from which it is natural to infer that the African versions are older and nearer to the original than the corresponding but incomplete narratives in Genesis." (Frazer's "Worship of Nature," pp. 223-224.)

The hypothetical first man of the Bible is rightly named Adam, since the word Adam, which means Man, was reputedly made out of Adamah, which means the Ground or Earth. Similarly among the ancient Romans, man was called Homo, because he was

supposedly made from Humus, the Earth. According
to an ancient Egyptian myth, Knoumou, the Father
of the Gods, moulded the earliest men out of clay on
a potter's wheel. We are informed by the Chaldean
priest, Berosus, that the great god Bel decapitated
himself, and that the other gods mixed his blood with
clay, and out of it fashioned the first man. In the
Greek mythology, Prometheus is depicted as manufacturing men from clay at Panopeus. (For scholarly
studies of these creation tales the curious reader is
referred to "Folklore in the Old Testament," by Sir
J. G. Frazer, and "Forgery in Christianity," by Major
Joseph Wheless.)

THE CHRIST MYTH

THE triumph of the doctrine of Evolution has recon-
ciled the more literate Christians to the non-historicity of Adam. As the historicity of Jesus, however,
is now widely questioned, even the most liberal de-
fenders of the faith find themselves in a very uncom-
fortable position, being belabored by both fundamen-
talists and ultrarationalists alike. After surrendering
the theological Christ, the liberal Christian apologist
finds out, much to his chagrin, that practically nothing is known about the historical Jesus. Our chief
sources of information concerning Jesus Christ are
the genuine Pauline Epistles and the Four Gospels of
the New Testament. There are also the alleged
references to Jesus by Jewish and Pagan writers, but
most of these are of extremely doubtful authenticity.
There is a famous passage in "The Antiquities of the
Jews," by Flavius Josephus, in which reference is
made to Jesus Christ, but it is generally regarded as
a forgery, even by Christian scholars. The passage
is not mentioned by any Christian writer before
Eusebius, in the early part of the 4th century. Tacitus,
the Roman historian, in his celebrated "Annals," refers
to the burning of Rome in 64 A. D. and the Neronian

persecution of the Christians. He describes them as a "vast multitude" and says that the cult was founded by Christus, who was punished as a criminal by the Procurator Pontius Pilate. Eusebius made a list of Jewish and Pagan references to Christianity, but Tacitus is not mentioned by him. In fact, the passage in question was not quoted by any Christian writer before the 15th century. Pliny the Younger, Proconsul of Bithynia, wrote a letter to the Roman Emperor Trajan (early 2nd century), in which he reported the presence in his province of a group of people who gathered before daybreak on a certain day and sang hymns to Christ as a god. There is no evidence that this Christ was the Jesus of the Gospels. The Emperor Hadrian in a letter to the Consul Servianus (A. D. 134), asserts that the worshippers of the sun-god Serapis, in Egypt, were Christians, and that these sun-worshippers called themselves "Bishops of Christ". The worship of Serapis was imported into Egypt from Pontus, a province bordering on Bithynia. The Christians mentioned by Pliny the Younger were in all probability worshippers of Serapis.

Suetonius in his "Life of Claudius", relates that: "He (Claudius) drove the Jews, who at the instigation of Chrestus were constantly rioting, out of Rome." This is said to have taken place about 15 years after the crucifixion of Jesus. So Chrestus could hardly have been Jesus Christ. Philo, an eminent Jewish philosopher and historian, was a contemporary of Jesus. He wrote the history of the Jews of the time of Christ, but makes no mention of Jesus. Philo developed the doctrine of the Logos, and although according to Christian theology Jesus Christ was the Logos, he was not aware of the identity. Justus of Tiberias, a native of Galilee, wrote a history covering the period in which Jesus is said to have lived, but does not in any instance call the name of the Christ. The works of Justus have now all perished, but they were read by Photius, a Christian Bishop and scholar, of Constantinople (9th century). Says Photius: "He (Justus) makes not the least mention of the appearance of Christ, of what things happened to him, or of the wonderful work that he did." The paucity of our information concerning the Christian savior is concisely expressed by Mr. Robert Keable, in his work, "The Great Galilean":

"No man knows sufficient of the early life of Jesus to write a biography of him. For that matter, no one knows enough for the normal Times obituary notice of a great man. If regard were had to what we should call, in correct speech, definitely historical facts, scarcely three lines could be filled. Moreover, if newspapers had been in existence, and if that obituary notice had had to be written in the year of his death, no editor could have found in the literature of his day so much as his name. Yet few periods of the ancient world were so well documented as the period of Augustus and Tiberius. But no contemporary knew of his existence. Even a generation later, a spurious passage in Josephus, a questionable reference in Suetonius, and the mention of a name that may be his by Tacitus—that is all. His first mention in any surviving document, secular or religious, is 20 years after."

The genuine Pauline Epistles, in the New Testament, are Romans, I and II Corinthians and Galatians. The other letters attributed to St. Paul are regarded as spurious. The genuine Epistles were written from about 52 to 64 A. C. (After Christ). The dates of origin of the Four Gospels have been estimated as follows: Mark—70 to 100 A. C. Luke—about 100 A. C. Matthew—100 to 110 A. C. John—sometime between 100 and 160 A. C. That these Gospel stories are replete with inaccuracies and contradictions is obvious to all who read with a discerning eye. In Matthew II, 1, we are told that Jesus Christ was born "in the days of Herod." But in Luke II, 1-7, we are told that the Christ child first saw the light of day, "when Cyrenius was governor of Syria". There is here a discrepancy of at least 10 years, for Herod died in the year 4 B. C., while Cyrenius, or Quirinius, as he is known in Roman history, did not become Governor of Syria until the year 7 A. C. According to the Rev. Dr. Giles, in his "Hebrew and Christian Records": "We have no clue to either the day or the time of year, or even the year itself, in which Chirst was born." Matthew 1: 6-16 lists 28 generations from David to Jesus while Luke 3:23-31 tabulates 43. According to John, Jesus visited Jerusalem at least 4 times, but the Synoptics (Mark, Luke and Matthew) assure us that he journeyed to that city only once. As to the length of the Lord's ministry the Synoptics say one year but John says at least 3 years. From the Synoptical account, we gather that the Savior carried on his work chiefly in Galilee, but John informs us that Judea was the principal theater of the ministry of Christ. The hour of the crucifixion is likewise uncertain. One account fixes the time at the 3rd hour (9 A.M.), Mark 15:25. Another account says it occurred at about the 6th hour (Noon), Luke 23:44. It is alleged that Jesus predicted that he would sojourn in the tomb for three days and three nights, Mat. 12:40. But in the Synoptic accounts of the event as it is said to have actually happened, the time is given as two nights and one day, i. e., one day and a half. Should we inquire as to who visited the tomb first, we receive four different answers. John says one woman; Matthew, two women; Mark, three women; and Luke, a crowd of women. When we ask whom did the women meet at the tomb, we again receive four replies. Matthew asserts that they saw one angel, whereas Mark declares it was one young man. According to Luke, the women saw two men. And John says that they saw two angels. These women also saw Jesus, if we believe Matthew (28th chapter). If we give credence to Luke (24th chapter), the women did not see Jesus. Nor do these inspired scribes display unanimity regarding the number of days between the resurrection and the ascension. The elapsed time was only one day, if we follow Luke, and at least 10 days if we take the word of John. The Book of Acts extends the period to 40 days. Since both the Gospel according to Luke and the Book of Acts are said to have been written by the author, these discrepancies are very puzzling, to say the least. According to Holy Writ, Jesus the Christ terminated his earthly pilgrimage by ascending to heaven. The exact location of his departure, it seems, is unknown. The ascension took place in Jerusalem, if Mark wrote correctly. Not so, if Luke knew whereof he spoke, for he relates that it was at Bethany. The Book of Acts gives Mt. Olivet as the scene of the momentous event. Let it be noted that Matthew and John make no mention of the ascension; that it occurs in Mark in the Spurious Addendum (the last 12 verses, which were not in the original manuscript), and that Luke's version does not appear in the Codex Sinaiticus, a 4th century manuscript now in the British Museum. The Gospel writers advance three views as to the nature of Jesus. Mark regards him as the Son of Man. Matthew and Luke hail him as the Son of God, while John recognizes him as God Himself.

A consideration of Pagan parallels will put the Gospel records in a clearer light. Let us become as little children, and travel backwards in time, with a venerable Bishop as our guide:

"Suppose you had been a child living in Rome 1940 years ago; that is, a few years before Jesus is supposed to have been born. About a week before December 25th, you would have found everybody preparing for a great feast, just as they do in Europe today. To those Romans December 25th was the birthday of the sun. They wrote that in gold letters in their calendars. Every year about that time, the middle of winter, the sun was born once more and it was going to put an end to the darkness and misery of winter. So they had a great feast, with presents and dolls for everybody, and the best day of all was December 25th. That feast, they would tell you, was thousands of years old. . . . Just outside Rome there was an underground temple of the Persian God Mithra. Well, at midnight, the first minute of December 25th, you would have seen that temple all lit up with candles, and priests in white garments at the altar, and boys burning incense; exactly as you will see in a Roman Catholic church at midnight on December 24th in our own time. And the worshippers of Mithra would have told you that Mithra was a good God who had come from heaven to be born as man and redeem men from their sins; and he was born in a dark cave or stable on December 25th.

"Then suppose you had asked somebody where the Egyptians who lived in Rome had their temple. You would have found these also celebrating the birth of their savior-god Horus, who was born of a virgin in a stable on December 25th. In the temple you would find a statue or figure of the infant-god Horus lying in a manger, and a statue of his virgin-mother Isis standing beside it; just as in a Roman Catholic Church on Christmas day you will find a stable or cave rigged up and the infant Jesus in a manger and a figure of Mary beside it.

"Then you might go to the Greek temple, and find them paying respect to the figure of their savior-god in a manger or cradle. And if you found the quarters of the gladiators, the war-captives from Germany, you would have found these also holding a feast, and they would explain that December 25th (or midwinter) was, all over Europe, the great feast of Yule, or the Wheel, which means that the sun had turned back, like a wheel, and was going once more to redeem men from the hell of winter to the heaven of summer." (*Science and History for Girls and Boys*, Galion, Ohio, 1932, pp. 138-139, by Bishop William Montgomery Brown. This book is addressed to a juvenile audience, but it is a very able work, and can be read with profit by intelligent adults.)

PAGAN CHRISTS

THE Egyptian analogies to the Christian Epic are so close in some cases as to suggest an Egyptian origin for certain Christian doctrines and rites. This is clearly shown by Gerald Massey:

"The Christian dispensation is believed to have been ushered in by the birth of a child, and the portrait of that child in the Roman Catacombs as the child of Mary is the youthful Sun-God in the Mummy Image of the child-king, the Egyptian Karast, or Christ. The alleged facts of our Lord's life as Jesus the Christ, were equally the alleged facts of our Lord's life as the Horus of Egypt, whose very name signifies the Lord. . . . The Jesus Christ with female paps, who is the Alpha and Omega of Revelation, was the Iu of Egypt, and the Iao of the Chaldeans. Jesus as the Lamb of God, and Ichthys the Fish, was Egyptian. Jesus as the Coming One; Jesus born of the Virgin Mother, who was overshadowed by the Holy Ghost, Jesus born of two mothers, both of whose names are Mary; Jesus born in the manger—at Christmas, and again at Easter; Jesus saluted by the three kings, or Magi; Jesus of the transfiguration on the Mount; Jesus whose symbol in the Catacombs is the eight-rayed Star—the Star of the East; Jesus as the eternal Child; Jesus as God the Father, re-born as his own Son; Jesus as the child of twelve years; Jesus as the Anointed One of thirty years; Jesus in his Baptism; Jesus walking on the Waters, or working his Miracles; Jesus as the Caster-out of demons; Jesus as a Substitute, who suffered in a vicarious atonement for sinful men; Jesus whose followers are the two bretheren, the four fishers, the seven fishers, the twelve apostles, the seventy (or seventy-two in some texts) whose names were written in Heaven; Jesus who was administered to by seven women; Jesus in his bloody sweat; Jesus betrayed by Judas; Jesus as Conqueror of the grave; Jesus the Resurrection and the Life; Jesus before Herod; in the Hades, and in his re-appearance to the women. and to the seven fishers; Jesus who was crucified both on the 14th and 15th of the month Nisan; Jesus who was also crucified in Egypt (as it is written in Revelation); Jesus as Judge of the Dead, with the sheep on the right, and the goats on the left, is Egyptian from first to last, in every phase. from the beginning to the end." (*Historical Jesus and Mythical Christ*, pp. 42-44, London, 1936. For an exhaustive treatment, see Massey's *Natural Genesis*. 2 vols. Other valuable references are Samuel Sharpe's *Egyptian Mythology*, Bonwick's *Egyptian Belief and Modern Thought*, Frazer's *Adonis, Attis, Osiris*, and Doane's *Bible Myths*.)

Osiris, the father of Horus, was another virgin-born god of ancient Egypt. His Sufferings, Death and Resurrection were celebrated in an annual Mystery-Play at Abydos, on about March 25th, an approximation of the Vernal Equinox, i.e., Easter. The Pharoah Amenhotep III, of the 17th dynasty, was hailed as the son of the virgin Mutemua. His birth is pictured on the inner walls of the Temple of Amen in Thebes. "In this picture", declares the Egyptologist, Samuel Sharpe, "we have the Annunciation, the Conception, the Birth and the Adoration, as described in the first and second chapters of Luke's gospel; and as we have historical assurance that the chapters in Matthew's gospel which contain the miraculous birth are an after addition not in the earliest manuscripts, it seems probable that these two poetical chapters in Luke may also be unhistorical, and borrowed from the Egyptian accounts of the miraculous births of their kings."

Another great Pagan Christ was Krishna of India. In the sacred books of India it is recorded that Krishna was born of the virgin Devaki, that his nativity was heralded by a Star, and that though of royal lineage, he was born in a Cave. (According to the Apocryphal Gospel of Protevangelion, a work attributed to James the brother of Jesus, the Christian Savior was born in a cave.) At the time of Krishna's birth, the cave was mysteriously illuminated. (At the birth of Jesus, "there was a great light in the cave, so that the eyes of Joseph and the Midwife could not bear it."—New Testament Apocrypha:—Protevangelion.) The infant Krishna spoke to his mother soon after his birth. ("Jesus spake even when he was in the cradle, and said to his mother:—'Mary I am Jesus the Son of God, that Word which thou did bring forth according to the declaration of the Angel Gabriel unto thee, and my Father hath sent me for the salvation of the world.' "—N. T. Apocrypha:—Gospel of the Infancy.) Krishna was born while his foster-father Nanda was in the city to pay his tax to the King. (Jesus was born while his foster-father Joseph was in the city to pay his tax to the Governor:—New Testament:—Gospel of Luke.) The babe Krishna was adored by Cowherds. (The infant Jesus was adored by Shepherds.) King Kansa sought the life of the Indian Christ by ordering the massacre of all male children born during the same night as was Krishna. (This is almost identical with the story of the slaughter of the innocents, ordered by Herod, according to Matthew, II.) Nanda was warned by a heavenly voice to flee with the infant Krishna across the Jumna River, to Gakul, to escape King Kansa. (Joseph was warned by a voice in a dream to flee into Egypt with the Christ-child to escape the wrath of Herod.) Krishna performed many miracles in the city of Mathura. (Jesus, while in Egypt, lived in a town named Matarea, where he performed many miracles.) Krishna was a crucified Christ. He is pictured in Indian art as hanging on a cross with arms extended. (Dr. Thomas Inman a celebrated authority on Pagan and Christian symbolism, states that: "Krishna whose history so closely resembles our Lord's, was also like him in his being crucified."—Cited by T. W. Doane, in his "Bible Myths", p. 186, N. Y., 1910). Krishna was pierced by an arrow while hanging on the cross. (Jesus was pierced by a spear during his crucifixion.) The light of the sun was blotted out at noon on the day of Krishna's death. (The sun was darkened from the 6th to the 9th hour on the day of the crucifixion of Christ.) Krishna descended into hell to raise the dead before returning to the abode of the gods. (We read of Jesus Christ that:—"He descended into hell, and on the third day rose again from the dead." The Descent into Hell of Christ is described in the apocryphal Gospel of Nicodemus.) Krishna rose from the grave, and finally ascended bodily to heaven in the presence of a multitude of spectators. (A similar story is related of Jesus Christ.) In Indian art Krishna is represented as a man of black complexion. The word Krishna, literally means The Black. (In early Christian art Jesus is almost invariably represented as a black man.) Sir Godfrey Higgins made a thorough investigation of the pictures and images of black Infants and Madonnas in the cathedrals of Europe. "In all the Romish countries of Europe," says he, "France, Italy, Germany, etc., the God Christ, as well as his mother, are described in their old pictures to be black. The infant God in the arms of his black mother, his eyes and drapery white, is himself perfectly black. If the reader doubt my word he may go to the cathedral at Moulins, to the famous Chapel of the Virgin at Loretto, to the Church of the Annunciata, the church at St. Lazaro or the Church of St. Stephen at Genoa, to St. Francisco at Pisa, to the church at Brixen in Tyrol and to that at Padua, to Church of

St. Theodore at Munich, to a church and to the Cathedral at Augsburg, where a black virgin and child as large as life, to Rome and the Borghese Chapel of Maria Maggiore, to the Pantheon, to a small chapel of St. Peters on the right hand side on entering, near the door; and in fact, to almost innumerable other churches in countries professing the Romish religion. There is scarcely an old church in Italy where some remains of the worship of the black virgin and black child are not to be met with. Very often the black figures have given place to white ones, and in these cases the black ones, as being held sacred, were put into retired places in the churches, but were not destroyed, and are yet to be found there. . . . When the circumstance has been named to the Romish priests they have endeavored to disguise the fact by pretending that the child had become black by the smoke of candles; but it was black where the smoke of a candle never came, and besides, how came the candles not to blacken the white of the eyes, the teeth and the shirt, and to redden the lips? Their real blackness is not to be questioned. . . . A black virgin and child among the white Germans, Swiss, French and Italians." (The Anacalypsis, Vol. I, Book IV, Chap. I, by Sir Godfrey Higgins.) Krishna was the second person in the Hindu Trinity, which consisted of:— (1) Brahma, (2) Vishnu and (3) Siva. Krishna was the human incarnation of Vishnu. (Jesus Christ is considered to be the second person in the Christian Trinity.)

The close parallels between the life-stories of Buddha and Christ are just as remarkable as those between Krishna and Christ. Buddha was born of a virgin named Maya, or Mary. His birthday was celebrated on Dec. 25th. He was visited by wise men who acknowledged his divinity. The life of Buddha was sought by King Bimbasara, who feared that some day the child would endanger his throne. At the age of twelve, Buddha excelled the learned men of the temple in knowledge and wisdom. His ancestry was traced back to Maha Sammata, the first monarch in the world. (Jesus' ancestry is traced back to Adam, the first man in the world.) Buddha was tempted by Mara (the Author of Evil), who said:—"Go not forth to adopt a religious life and in seven days thou shalt become an emperor of the world." Buddha replied:— "Get thee away from me." Also, Buddha was transfigured on a mountain top. His form was illumined by an aura of bright light. (Jesus was likewise transfigured on a mountain top. "And his face did shine as the sun, and his raiment was white as the light."— Matt. XVII, 1-2.) After the completion of his earthly mission, Buddha ascended bodily to the celestial realms.

Mithra, a Persian sun-god, was virgin-born, in a cave, on Dec. 25th. His earliest worshippers were shepherds, and he was accompanied in his travels by 12 companions. The Mithraists kept the sabbath day holy, and celebrated the Eucharist by eating wafers embellished with a cross. The great Mithraic festivals were the Birth (Christmas) and the Resurrection (Easter).

Adonis or Tammuz of Babylonia, was also born of a virgin. He died a cruel death, descended into hell, arose from the tomb and ascended to heaven. In a mid-summer festival, the worshippers of Adonis wept over an effigy of the dead god, which was washed with water, anointed with oil and clothed in red robes, amid clouds of incense. On the next day the Resurrection was re-enacted, after which the crowd shouted:—"The Lord is Risen." Finally his ascension was simulated in the presence of his devotees.

Attis of Phrygia was called the Good Shepherd, and was said to be the son of the virgin Nana. It is reported that Attis, when in his prime, mutilated himself and bled to death under a sacred pine tree. The

Festivals of the Death and Resurrection of Attis were staged by his worshippers from March 22nd through March 25th. A pine tree was cut on March 22nd, and an image of the god was tied to the trunk. He was shown as "slain and hanged on a tree." (Cf. New Testament:—Acts, V, 30.) Then the effigy was buried in a tomb. On the night of March 24th, the priests opened the tomb and found it empty. The Resurrection of Attis was celebrated on March 25th. His followers were baptized in blood, thereby having their sins washed away, and they were therefore declared to have been "born again."

Strange as it may seem, the Aztecs of ancient Mexico likewise could boast of a crucified savior. Quetzalcoatl was born of a virgin, and also, like Jesus, was tempted and fasted for forty days. He is shown in the Borgian Ms., on a cross, with nail marks on his hands and feet. He is depicted as a man of sable hue. After being crucified, he rose from the dead and went into the East. The Mexicans were expecting his Second Coming when the Spaniards invaded the country in the 16th century.

SOURCES OF THE CHRIST MYTH

THERE are two principal types of savior-gods recognized by hierologists, namely: vegetation-gods and sun-gods. The vegetation theory has been brilliantly developed by Sir J. G. Frazer, in his "Golden Bough," and by Grant Allen in "The Evolution of the Idea of God." This viewpoint is concisely summarized by the noted psychologist Dr. David Forsyth:

"Many gods besides Christ have been supposed to die, be resurrected and ascend to heaven. This idea has now been traced back to its origin among primitive people in the annual death and resurrection of crops and plant life generally. This explains the world-wide prevalence of the notion. Among still more primitive tribes, as Grant Allen showed, it is not yet understood that sown corn sprouts because of the spring sunshine, and they attribute the result to divine agency. To this end they are accustomed at seed time to kill their tribal god—either in human or animal form—and scatter the flesh and the blood over the sown fields. They believe that the seeds will not grow unless the god is sacrificed and added to them in this manner. When, therefore, the crop appears, they never doubt that it is their god coming to life again. It is from this erroneous belief of primitive tribes that Christianity today derives its belief in Christ's Death and Resurrection." ("Psychology and Religion," p. 97, by David Forsyth, London, 1935.)

According to the advocates of the solar myth theory, the ancient crucified saviors were personifications of the sun, and their life-stories were allegories of the sun's passage through the twelve constellations of the Zodiac. This hypothesis is ably presented in the following works: "The Ruins of Empires," by Count Volney, Barlow's translation, published by Peter Eckler, New York, 1890; "The Origin of All Religious Worship," by Charles F. Dupuis, New Orleans, 1872; "Pagan and Christian Creeds," by Edward Carpenter; "Pagan Christs" and "Christianity and Mythology," by John M. Robertson; "The Natural Genesis," by Gerald Massey; "The Christ Myth," by Professor Arthur Drews; "Bible Myths," by T. W. Doane; and "The Eliminator," by Rev. Dr. Richard B. Westbrook. The astronomical elements in the Christian Epic are pointed out by Edward Carpenter with characteristic lucidity:

"The Passover, the greatest feast of the Jews, borrowed from the Egyptians, handed down to become the supreme festival of Christianity, . . . is, as well known, closely connected with the celebration of the Spring Equinox and of the passing over of the Sun from south to north of the equator, i.e., from his winter depression to his summer dominion. The Sun, at the moment of passing the equinoctial point, stood 3,000 years ago in the zodiacal constellation of the Ram, or he-lamb. The Lamb, therefore, became the symbol of the young triumphant god. . . . At an earlier date—owing to the precession of the equinoxes— the Sun at the spring passage stood in the constellation of the Bull; so, in the older worships of Egypt, and of Persia and of India, it was the Bull that was sacred and the symbol of the god. . . . In the representation of the Zodiac in the Temple of Denderah (in Egypt) the figure of Virgo is annotated by a smaller figure of Isis with Horus in her arms; and the Roman Church fixed the celebration of Mary's assumption into the glory at the very date (15th August) of the said constellation's disappearance from sight in the blaze of the solar rays, and her birth on the date (8th Sept.) of the same constellation's reappearance. . . . Jesus himself . . . is purported to have been born like the other sungods, Bacchus, Apollo, Osiris, on the 25th day of December, the day of the Sun's rebirth, i.e., the first day which obviously lengthens after the 21st of December." ("Love's Coming of Age," pp. 146-149, New York, 1926.)

Vegetation cults, it seems, are older than stellar or solar cults, but were later blended with them. In the primitive vegetation-god sacrifice, the victim was, it is believed, originally the King, or head-man, of the tribe or clan. It was believed by ancient man that the prosperity of the tribe depended on the well-being of the ruler. If the king became old and feeble, it was considered a foregone conclusion that the nation or tribe would suffer a similar decline. So the king, who was usually regarded as a god in human form, was sacrificed, and replaced with a younger and more vigorous man. After much passage of time, the son of the king was substituted in the sacrificial rite, and being also the offspring of divinity, he was properly called the son of the god. At a still later period, a condemned criminal was chosen in the place of the royal victim. This culprit was given regal honors for a time, then put to death. He was generally slain while bound to a sacred tree, with arms outstretched in the form of a cross. After being entombed, he was believed to rise from the dead within three days; the three-day period representing the return of vegetation. The question naturally arises: — Why three days? The answer is, that the three-day period is based on the 3-day interval between the Old and New Moons. (See Frazer's "Folklore in the Old Testament," abridged edition, p. 29, New York, 1927.) It is still believed by certain persons of a superstitious type that there is an intimate connection between the phases of the moon and the growth of crops.

According to the Chaldean historian, Berosus, there was a religious festival celebrated annually in ancient Babylon, known as the Sacaea. The duration of the fete was five days, and for that length of time servants and masters exchanged places in society, the servants giving orders and the masters obeying them. The King temporarily abdicated the throne, and a mock-king called Zoganes reigned in his place. But after the five days were over, the mock-king was dethroned and scourged, and then either hanged or crucified. An eminent Egyptologist has noted that: "The victims of these human sacrifices were generally crucified, or else killed and then 'hung on a tree' until the evening. In this regard it is interesting to notice that in the Acts the writer mistakenly speaks of Jesus as having been slain and then hanged on a tree, as though this were a common phrase coming readily to his mind; and the word 'hanged' is frequently used in Greek to denote crucifixion." ("The Paganism in Our Christianity," pp. 77-78, by Sir Arthur Weigall, New York and London, 1928.)

Among the advocates of the non-historicity of Jesus, John M. Robertson and L. Gordon Rylands are

widely known. In his "Evolution of Christianity,"
Mr. Rylands contends that the name Jesus is the
Greek equivalent of the Hebrew Joshua. Joshua,
it seems, was an ancient Hebrew sun-god, who was
demoted to the status of a man by the priests of the
Yahweh cult. However, the worship of Joshua was
continued in secret by his devotees, until the fall of
Jerusalem. After that event, secrecy was no longer
necessary, so that the Joshua cult again came out
into the open. The sacrificed Jesus, or Joshua, according to Robertson and Rylands, was not a historical personage, but a character in a Mystery-Play.
"What is clear," declares Mr. Robertson, "is that the
central narrative of the gospel biography, the story of
the Last Supper, the Agony, Betrayal, Trial and Crucifixion, is neither a contemporary report nor a historical tradition, but the simple transcript of a Mys-
tery-Drama." ("A Short History of Christianity,"
p. 9, by J. M. Robertson, London, 1931.) The views
of Rylands and Robertson have been challenged by
Joseph McCabe and Sir Arthur Weigall. Mr. Mc-
Cabe holds that it is more reasonable to conclude from
the available evidence that Jesus did actually live;
that he was a man who was gradually turned into a
god. Sir Arthur Weigall counters the mythicists
with a very ingenious theory. According to Sir Arthur, when Jesus was crucified he did not die, but
only swooned; and that afterwards he was revived
by his friends and spirited away. The Matthew nar-
rator tells us that the chief priests and Pharisees re-
quested Pilate to station a guard of Roman soldiers
at the tomb of Jesus: "Lest his disciples come by night
and steal him away, and say unto the people, he is
risen from the dead." It is stated in the Bible account
that the guard was not placed at the tomb until the
second night after the burial of Jesus. Weigall sug-
gests that the Christ was taken out of the tomb on
the first night; so that the soldiers stood watch over

an empty sepulchre. Since the report was abroad that Jesus had died on the cross, accounts of subsequent appearances must have convinced many persons that he had risen from the dead. The myths and legends concerning such Pagan Christs as Osiris, Horus, Adonis, Krishna, etc., were later interpolated into the biography of Jesus. The famous dramatist, George Moore, in his play "The Apostle," also depicts Jesus as surviving the crucifixion. Finally Paul meets Jesus in a monastery, whence Jesus had fled into exile. When Paul discovered that Jesus had not died on the cross, and as a result had not risen from the dead, he became furious, and in a fit of temper, slew Jesus. This is a symbolic way of showing that historic Christianity is based on the teachings of St. Paul rather than on those of Jesus; that the influence of Paul triumphed over that of Jesus in the early church.

Whether Jesus lived or not, we may conclude with certainty, that Christianity is of Pagan origin. December the 25th is celebrated as the birthday of Jesus Christ. This date is an approximation of the Winter Solstice, and the birthday of several Pagan sun-gods. Its pagan derivation is beyond all dispute. "The Gospels say nothing as to the day of Christ's birth," declares Sir J. G. Frazer, "and accordingly the early church did not celebrate it. In time, however, the Christians of Egypt came to regard the 6th of January as the date of the Nativity, and the custom of commemorating the birth of the Savior on that day gradually spread until by the 4th century it was universally established in the East. But at the end of 3rd or the beginning of the 4th century the Western Church, which had never recognized the 6th of January as the day of the Nativity, adopted the 25th of December as the true date, and in time its decision was accepted also by the Eastern Church." ("The Golden Bough," abridged edition, p. 358, London,

1932.) The reason why the change was made is best stated by an ancient Syrian writer, who was himself a Christian. Says he: "The reason why the fathers transferred the celebration of the 6th of January to the 25th of December was this. It was a custom of the heathen to celebrate on the same 25th of December the birthday of the Sun, at which time they kindled lights in token of festivity. In these solemnities and festivities the Christians also took part. Accordingly when the doctors of the Church perceived that the Christians had a leaning to this festival, they took counsel and resolved that the true Nativity should be solemnized on that day and the festival of the Epiphany on the 6th of January. Accordingly, along with this custom, the practice has prevailed of kindling fires till the sixth." Easter is likewise of heathen origin. It is an approximation of the Vernal Equinox. Easter falls on the first Sunday after the first full moon after the Vernal Equinox (the 21st of March), and it may come as early as the 22nd of March, or as late as the 25th of April. The very name of the festival betrays its pagan source, for Easter is a variant of Eostre or Ostara, the name of the Anglo-Saxon goddess of Spring. The Festival of St. George takes place on April 23rd. It is a Christian replica of the ancient Parilia, or Birthday of Rome. St. George was originally the Egyptian god, Horus, who slew the Egyptian devil, Set, in the form of a Dragon. The Festival of All Souls is a Christian copy of the ancient Egyptian Feast of the Lamps, and as Weigall observes: "Christians unconsciously perpetuate the worship of Osiris and the commemoration of all his subjects in the Kingdom of the Dead." ("The Paganism in Our Christianity," p. 127.)

The mysterious doctrine of the Trinity loses the character of mystery when we consider its origin. In ancient Egypt the Sun was worshipped as a god. Since there can be no life without sunlight, the Sun was recognized as the Creator of life, and since without adequate sunlight living things wither and die, the Sun was regarded as the Protector, or preserver of life. An excess of sunlight destroys life, so that the Sun was also known as the Destroyer of life. The Sun, considered in its three aspects of Creator, Protector and Destroyer, was indeed a Trinity in Unity. Solar and stellar symbolism have profoundly affected the Christian religion. For instance, in the Apocalypse, we read of the Four Beasts and the Four Horsemen. Taken literally the narrative does not make sense, but when we learn that the beasts are zodiacal constellations and the horsemen, planets, we get a much clearer perception of the matter. In Revelation 4:7, we read that: "the first beast was like a lion, and the second beast like a calf, and the third beast had a face as a man, and the fourth beast was like a flying eagle." These animals were the constellations that were situated at the four cardinal points of the Zodiac 5,000 years ago. They were Taurus the Bull (Vernal Equinox), Leo the Lion (Summer Solstice), Scorpio the Scorpion (Autumnal Equinox) and Aquarius the Waterman (Winter Solstice). The reader will notice that in the Bible the Eagle has been substituted for the Scorpion. According to Sir Godfrey Higgins: "The signs of the zodiac with the exception of the Scorpion, which was exchanged by Dan for the Eagle, were carried by the different tribes of the Israelites on their standards; and Taurus, Leo, Aquarius and Scorpio or the Eagle, the four signs of Reuben, Judah, Ephriam and Dan, were placed at the four corners of their encampment, evidently in allusion to the cardinal points of the sphere, the equinoxes and solstices." Now for the Horsemen and their steeds. The first horseman is a conqueror, armed with a bow and wearing a crown, and riding a white horse. (This is the planet Venus.) The second horse is red, and on it is a warrior with a sword. (The red planet is of course Mars, worshipped by the ancients as the god of war.) The third horse is black, (the planet Saturn), and his rider holds a pair of balances aloft. (The balances may be emblematic of the zodiacal constellation Libra, for the sun was in that constellation when day and night were equal, just as though weighed on a pair of scale pans.) The fourth horse is of a pale complexion (pale green or blue-green, the color of the planet Mercury), and astride him sits Death. (The ancient Babylonians built their temples in seven stages, each of a different color, representing the sun, the moon, and the five planets visible to the naked eye. The colors of the four horses point to their origin in the astrological lore of Babylonia.)

The sacred monogram Chi-Rho, so called because composed of the Greek letters chi(X) and rho(P), is of Egyptian origin. According to Sir Flinders Petrie, the Egyptologist, the monogram Chi-Rho was the emblem of the Egyptian god, Horus, thousands of years before Christ. The letters IHS constitute another sacred monogram of Christ. These letters were also the sacred symbol of the Greek sun-god Bacchus, or Dionysus. The Christians adopted them as they did many other symbols from the pagans. These letters form the root of the name JESUS. IHS when translated from Greek to Latin becomes IES. Adding the Latin masculine suffix, US, we get IES plus US, which equals IESUS. In English the I becomes J, hence we get JESUS.

Many incidents of the Gospel stories can be explained only as myths. We read of Satan leading Jesus to the mountain top. The devil has been represented in Jewish and Christian folklore and art in the form of a goat. We see Satan in Medieval paintings with the hooves, horns, and tail of a goat. The Greek god Pan was part goat, and is represented as leading Zeus to the mountain top. In ancient Babylon the Goat was the emblem of the zodiacal constellation

Capricorn. The sun reached the lowest point in the celestial sphere in this constellation, after which it began to climb toward the highest point. So the goat-god is imagined to lead the sun-god toward the highest point, figuratively called the mountain top. In Greek mythology we read of the savior Dionysus riding upon two asses, which afterwards he had changed into celestial constellations. Jesus is pictured as riding Jerusalem upon two asses, i.e., upon an ass and colt, the foal of an ass. (See Matthew 21:5-7.) In Babylonia the symbol of the zodiacal constellation Cancer, in which the sun reached the highest point of its apparent path, was the ASS and FOAL.

The signs and constellations of the Zodiac have been referred to several times in this essay, so it is advisable that we consider their origin and meaning. The Zodiac is an imaginary band encircling the celestial sphere. It stretches eight degrees on each side of the Ecliptic, the apparent path of the sun. The zodiac is divided into 12 equal sections, each corresponding to one month. Due to the annual revolution of the earth, the sun appears to make one complete circuit through the zodiac in one year, staying in each sign one month. The signs of the zodiac and the constellations of the zodiac were originally the same, but due to the precession of the equinoxes, each sign moves westward into the next constellation in about 2155 years. A sign therefore makes a complete circuit of the heavens in about 26,000 years. We are told by Professor Harding, the noted astronomer and mathematician, that the signs and constellations of the zodiac coincided about 300 B.C., and before that about 26,000 B.C. Since they were widely known thousands of years before 300 B.C., they evidently originated not later than about 26,000 B.C. (See Professor Arthur M. Harding's "Astronomy," Garden City, 1935.) The constellations of the zodiac have the following names: Aries (the Ram or Lamb), Taurus (the Bull or Ox), Gemini (the Twins), Cancer (the Crab), Leo (the Lion), Virgo (the Virgin), Libra (the Balances),. Scorpio (the Scorpion), Saggitarius (the Archer), Capricornus (the Goat), Aquarius (the Water-carrier), and Pisces (the Fishes). The following speculations on the origin of the names of the constellations are about as accurate as any list which might be compiled, the majority of students of the subject being in general agreement upon them. The constellations of the Lamb, the Bull and the Twins, were star-groups through which the sun passed in the spring; in which time of the year occurred the seasons of sheep-raising, ploughing and goat-breeding. The Twins were originally the two kids, since the young of goats are frequently born two at a time. The Crab was so called because the sun reached its most northern point in that constellation, and then returned toward the south, figuratively moving backward like a crab. The Lion is the star-group through which the sun moved in July, when its heat was most powerful, being compared with the most ferocious of the beasts. The Virgin is an emblem of the harvest season, when the young girls were sent out to glean in the fields. The Balance is the constellation in which the sun moved when day and night were equal in length, just as if they were weighed in a balance. The stars of the Scorpion were hidden by the sun during the season of unhealthy weather and of plagues, which were imagined to strike like a scorpion. Stars called the Archer reigned over the hunting season, when the hunter shot game with the bow and arrow. In the Goat the sun reached the lowest point in its course, after which it began to climb toward the north again, just as the wild goat climbs toward the summit of the hill. The Water-Carrier marked the position of the solar orb during the rainy season. The stars of the Fishes constituted that group through which the sun passed when the fishing season was at its height.

Many learned Christian scholars do not believe that Jesus had any idea of starting a new religion or of establishing a church. They believe that the real founder of institutional Christianity was St. Paul. Yet we read of Jesus referring to Peter as the rock upon which the church is to be built. St. Peter is also popularly represented as the gate-keeper of heaven. The name Peter comes from the Greek word Petra, which means Rock. This may be a pseudonym, since he is also referred to as Simon called Peter. That is, he may have been named Simon, and was called the Rock because of some trait of character, just as General Stonewall Jackson was so called because he stood up against the enemy like a stone wall. It is interesting to note that there was a popular Semitic god named Simon, and that the Egyptian god, Petra, was represented as being the door-keeper of heaven, the earth and the underworld.

In the Gospel of St. John, Jesus is presented in the office of the Judge of the Dead: "For the Father judgeth no man, but hath committed all judgment unto the Son." (John 5:22.) Osiris enacted this role in the Egyptian religion. He is shown on the monuments occupying the judgment seat, and holding the staff of authority and the crux ansata; and on his breast is a St. Andrew's cross. His throne is designed like a chess-board, the two colors representing the good and evil which come before him for judgment. The trial of the soul before Osiris in the Hall of Judgment is described in detail in the "Book of the Dead." According to the Hindus, Krishna will occupy the judgment seat on the last day.

As the stories of slain and risen gods are traced backward into the dim and distant past, we finally come to Africa. One of the oldest religious celebrations of the ancient Egyptians was the Sed Festival. Sir Flinders Petrie explains it as follows: "A special festival of the identity of the king with Osiris seems to have been celebrated every thirty years, and a greater festival of the same nature every one-hundred and twenty years. These periods are the lapse of a week and a month in the shifting calendar. The festival was called the sed or tail feast, as marking the end of a period. From the various representations, it has been gathered that at stated times the king was killed to prevent his old age impairing the fertility of the country, an African belief." ("Ancient Egyptians," p. 41, by Sir W. M. Flinders Petrie, Vol. No. 11, of Herbert Spencer's "Descriptive Sociology.") The earliest religion of Egypt has been traced back to Central Africa. "The oldest structure of the people," says Petrie, "was that which resembled the African in beliefs and practices. There is a large body of customs, especially those concerning the dead, which are closely alike in ancient Egypt and modern Central Africa. In this stratum, probably preceding 10,000 B.C., animal worship was usual; so strong was the primitive influence that this remained in practice down to the Roman age. The source of this was a sense of kinship of men and animals." ("The Gods of Ancient Egypt," in Hammerton's "Wonders of the Past," p. 667, New York, 1937.) The same high authority, Flinders Petrie, further states, "that the religion, like the population of Egypt, was always being mixed by successive migrations of invaders. The old African ideas which underlay it all still survive in Central Africa." (Ibid., p. 678.)

Limitations of both time and space prevent a more extended survey of this subject. The author hopes that some of the readers of this essay will find the time to make a critical study of Christian origins. Comparative religion is a fascinating study, and all students of human history should be well grounded in the fundamental principles of this important branch of social anthropology.

CPSIA information can be obtained
at www.ICGtesting.com
Printed in the USA
BVHW051254130223
658403BV00003B/417